THE
GOD
WHO
PURSUES

THE GOD WHO PURSUES

ENCOUNTERING A RELENTLESS GOD

CECIL MURPHEY

BETHANYHOUSE
MINNEAPOLIS, MINNESOTA

Published by Bethany House Publishers
A Ministry of Bethany Fellowship International
11400 Hampshire Avenue South
Bloomington, Minnesota 55438
www.bethanyhouse.com

Printed in the United States of America by
Bethany Press International, Bloomington, Minnesota 55438

Library of Congress Cataloging-in-Publication Data

Murphey, Cecil B.
    The God who pursues : encountering a relentless God / by Cecil Murphey.
        p.   cm.
    ISBN 0-7642-2586-3 (pbk.)
    1. Christian life—Presbyterian authors.   2. Holiness—Biblical teaching.
3. Bible. O.T.—Biography.   I. Title.
    BV4501.3 .M86   2002
    231.7—dc21   2002001527

IN APPRECIATION

- **Wanda and Randy Rosenberry, Cecile and Alan Hege, John Mark and Cathie Murphey:** You're family, but even more, I love you deeply.
- **David Morgan:** You have been my best friend through the darkest days and a joyful companion on the brightest.
- **Bible Discovery Sunday School Class:** You're the best class I've ever taught.
- **Carolyn Driver and the Christ Discipleship Ministries:** You've faithfully supported and encouraged me for several years. Thank you.
- **Steve Laube, senior editor at Bethany:** You encouraged me when few others did. I'll always be grateful for that.
- **Deidre Knight:** You've been more than a literary agent. You're also a friend and a mentoring spirit.
- **Shirley:** You know the reasons.

CONTENTS

THE DIVINE PURSUIT

Throughout my life, God has pursued me—relentlessly. I don't mean that God chased me until I surrendered and became a Christian. In fact, the initial awareness of that unmitigating pursuit began five years *after* my conversion. It was also the first time I became angry at God.

My experience began during my second year of college on a Monday, a day when I didn't have classes. I had sacrificed by not working full time so that I could study hard and serve God in ministry. On Tuesday, I faced a major final exam with two more finals later in the week; I had to spend the day preparing for those tests.

Shirley, my wife, woke up ill Monday morning and went back to bed. Our two preschool daughters weren't sick but were extremely fussy. As soon as I tried to focus on my studies, one or the other whimpered or commanded attention. If I stopped to take care of Wanda, Cecile demanded her share of time.

The mail arrived in the middle of the morning. Among the letters, I found our heating bill, for which we didn't have the money and wouldn't have it before it was due. We barely had enough groceries, and just enough gas in the car for me to drive to and from college the rest of the week. My car would soon need new brakes, and I had no idea how I could afford to have them replaced.

No matter what I did that morning to find study time, nothing improved. At least a dozen times I pleaded with God for help, adding, "I'm doing this so I can serve you better."

Despite my prayers, nothing changed at our house, other than that the girls fussed even more. By noon I had not studied more than three or four minutes at any one time. A headache came upon me suddenly, and I'm one of those people who rarely suffers such an affliction. It felt as if someone had stretched a heavy band around the top of my head and continued to tighten it.

Despite their crankiness, I fed Wanda and Cecile their lunch and put them down for a nap. My head ached so badly that I gave in and lay down on the sofa.

As quietness filled our house, I felt anything but peaceful. As I lay there, I reviewed my situation. I had grown tired of scraping money together every month and never having anything left over. Saving for bad days ahead was a joke; we were *living* in the bad days. My good friends at church were serving God while pursuing lucrative careers.

The tension had been building for weeks. No matter how carefully we managed our finances, unexpected expenses sneaked in. I thought, *I'm in debt because I'm studying to serve a God who won't provide money to pay my bills.* For perhaps ten minutes I grumbled about all of heaven's mistreatment. *Why am I serving God anyway? Others don't have these problems. None of my friends has to pray for money just to pay the bills.*

As my reasoning intensified, so did my anger. Then rage erupted: "I'm through with you, God!" I said aloud. "If you're all-powerful and all-loving, why don't you do something good for me? Why do you make it so hard to serve you?"

Instead of feeling better, the bitterness spewed out. "I don't believe in you any longer. What have I gotten from you except poverty and sacrifice? Besides, as a Christian I always have to seek guidance. Before my conversion, I just decided what I wanted and did it. That's the way I want to live from now on."

The more I thought of the freedom from checking in with God and waiting for guidance that didn't always come, the more I liked the idea.

"I'm through with Christianity."

Almost immediately, peace flooded me. I was free from God. I had made the decision; now I could divorce myself from any connection with the church or Jesus Christ. I would take my final exam the next day and the other two I had later in the week. After that, I would drop out of college and get a full-time job, perhaps continuing my education part time. I didn't want to serve God; I was finished with all of that religious business. I had tried it and it hadn't worked. It was time to enjoy my life and do what I wanted to do. I would never attend another church activity or read the Bible again.

But what about Wanda and Cecile?

That question burst from inside me. It was all right for me to choose not to follow God, but what about them?

"Shirley can take them to church if she wants to," I decided.

She's supposed to take over all the spiritual guidance?

Yes, I decided, she could do it. She would have to do it, because I was through with God. For five years I had sought God, and what good had it done me? I didn't want to think about God ever again. From now on I would focus on what I wanted. If the Bible should turn out to be true and I ended up in eternal torment, I didn't care. I just wanted to be free now.

What about your daughters? Do you have the right to treat them this way?

Then I exploded. If Shirley and the girls hadn't been asleep upstairs, I would have screamed at God so loudly that neighbors would have heard my roar.

"That isn't fair!"

God had smacked me with a sharp left hook. I didn't care about myself, but I couldn't gamble on the salvation of my girls. My anger intensified, and I told God so.

Just then I remembered an ad I had seen years earlier in a Christian magazine; an organization that reached out to alcoholics wanted financial support. The picture showed a man trapped inside a whiskey bottle. The agonized expression on his face, along with his outstretched hands, showed that he couldn't extricate himself from the bottle.

Yes, I thought, *that's just like me. I'm trapped. Penned in. God won't let me go no matter what I want.*

"What kind of God are you? I don't love you. I don't believe in you. I just want you out of my life! Why won't you let me alone?"

I don't know how long the railing continued, but for several minutes at least. Finally exhausted from all of my angry accusations, I stopped, too weary to fight any longer. "Okay, you've got me. I don't like it and I don't want you, but I can't turn away. Are you satisfied now?"

Of course, I heard no response.

"Even when I want to get away from you, you won't let me go, will you?"

As I listened to my own words, something clicked inside my head. Tears filled my eyes, and an overpowering sense of gratitude engulfed me. God would not let me go.

Even when I didn't want to follow, God still loved me and wanted me. I lay quietly, my eyes closed, and silently gave thanks for the unrelenting love that refused to let me run away.

As I continued to lie there, I heard a song, one that I was not aware of ever having heard before. A baritone sang, "O Jesus, I have promised to serve Thee to the end;/ Be Thou forever near me, my Master and my Friend./ I shall not fear the battle if Thou art by my side,/ Nor wander from the pathway if Thou wilt be my Guide." (John E. Bode, 1868, "O Jesus, I Have Promised," *The Hymnbook*, Presbyterian Church in the United States, 1965, 307.)

Then the tears flooded, and I begged for forgiveness. God wanted me so much that I could never pry loose the divine arms that hugged me tightly.

The end of the story is that both girls awakened alert, happy, and begged me, "Daddy, can we go outside and play?" I let them out into the front yard where I could see them enjoying themselves. For the next three hours—an unbelievably long time for them—they never came into the house. My headache disappeared as quickly as it had come. Shirley awakened in the middle of the afternoon and felt well enough to take over the girls' care. I studied for three solid hours. The next day I took the test and ended up with the highest grade in the class.

Finances still troubled us, but a few church friends, unaware of our needs, gave us money. Opportunities to speak in churches opened up, and each time I left with a handshake and an envelope with a check enclosed. We also paid the fuel bill a week before it was due.

My reason for sharing this story is that this was when I began to face the God Who Pursues—and pursues and pursues. One hymn captures this idea well: "O Love That Wilt Not Let Me Go . . ."

While writing this, I reviewed my history and became

aware of divine fingerprints smeared all over my life. Here are four instances.

(1) When I was eighteen months old, our loving family dog went berserk and mauled me. My mother told me years later that as she sat next to my bedside at the hospital, she was sure I would not survive, and that if I did, I'd be badly disfigured. She even asked God to take me. Of course, I did live, and although it took several plastic surgeries, little evidence remains today of that trauma. God was reaching for me even then and wouldn't let death claim me.

(2) Sunday school was an off-and-on experience for us kids. After almost a year of faithful attendance, I dropped out. One reason was that my teacher, Marie Garbie, wouldn't leave me alone. Almost every Sunday her dark eyes stared into mine, and she pointed a wrinkled, bony finger at me: "God's hand is on you. You're going to serve the Lord in a wonderful way. And I'm already claiming part of the reward because I've been your teacher."

I didn't want to serve the Lord. I didn't even know if I believed in Jesus Christ. I didn't care much anyway. I got uncomfortable and tired of hearing those words from her. I left her class, and I didn't open the door of a church for a full decade, and even then I sneaked inside. I know now that the Relentless God was in pursuit.

(3) Even my conversion experience reminds me of this aspect of the divine nature. At age sixteen, I learned the word *agnostic* and decided it fitted my thinking nicely. I didn't know if God existed, and I didn't care to explore the question; my

life functioned well without any heavenly interference. That is, until my early twenties, when a broken love affair threw my world upside down. She walked out of my life, and a deep sadness engulfed me that I couldn't escape. After several months of misery, I prayed for the first time in at least ten years: "If you are real, show yourself to me."

Nothing happened. I prayed those words three or four times, and nothing changed.

Just before midnight, while walking through town, I spotted a small church. I felt like a criminal, and I certainly didn't want anyone to see me, so I walked past the building three times. Then I tried the door, which was unlocked, and I rushed inside. They had left a dim light on in the foyer, as well as one in the worship area. I sat in a pew in the dark for several minutes, praying the only words I could: "If you're real, show me."

Again, nothing happened.

Feeling no better, I got up to leave. As I approached the door, I noticed a rack with New Testaments and a small sign: "Take One."

I did take one (I wasn't sure why) and put it in my pocket. The next day I began to read it, starting with "Abraham was the father of Isaac, and Isaac the father of Jacob . . ." and on and on for almost the entire first chapter of Matthew. I have no idea why I kept reading such a boring litany.

That is, I didn't know then. Today, I believe the Pursuing God was working steadily to get hold of me, yet I remained a fairly movable target.

I continued to read, and again, I can't explain why. Most of it didn't make sense to me, but I slowly moved from chapter to chapter. When I got to Romans, the theological arguments confused me. I couldn't define the reason, but even then I kept reading.

One day I reached Romans 10 and decided to stop forever, because nothing made sense. I started to close the New Testament, but my eyes fell on a verse: "Then Isaiah is so bold as to say, 'I have been found by those who did not seek me; I have shown myself to those who did not ask for me' " (RSV).

I read that several times before I realized something: I *believed* what I was reading. I couldn't have explained it or told anyone why; I simply knew that I believed. At that moment, the Relentless God grabbed me, and in the way that only the Divine Pursuer can work, I knew this was a message to me.

(4) My father was an alcoholic and so were my brothers. They're all dead because of that addiction (although all of them experienced God before they died). However, alcohol held no appeal for me. In my early twenties, I became a Christian.

Why? Why me? Why did it please God to pull me aside and chase me through my rebellious teens and finally pounce on me in my twenties? Did my brothers feel the same ruthless charge of God, yet drank to drown their awareness? I have no idea. I know only that God pursued me—and finally caught me.

These four experiences (and I could share others) convinced me that the All-Loving One has never stopped pursuing me. That's part of the joy and the pain of the Christian life. At times I still feel hemmed in, even when I suggest workable solutions to complex problems. I'm quick to point to paths to make the going easier, but the Divine Pursuer chases me down a different road.

The best way I can explain these divine pursuits is to begin with these words: *God is holy*. When we refer to God by that term, many of us immediately think of purity and righteousness. Or we cringe at words like *holy* by relegating them to old-fashioned, legalistic faith that prevents us from enjoying life. That's not the biblical concept.

In Scripture, *holy* means "totally different, separated, set apart for sacred use." In practical terms, it means that the Holy—the One who is completely other-than-human—tears the heavens apart, taps us on the shoulder, and whispers, "This is what I want you to see about yourself."

Church leaders used to call this process *sanctification*, meaning that God slowly molds us into the likeness of Jesus Christ by setting us aside, shaping us, affirming us, and even rebuking us. They used words such as *holiness*, but today we prefer terms like "growth" and "spiritual maturity."

Some of us have envisioned holiness (or spiritual maturity) as continuous acts of self-cleansing. We have to keep embracing rituals, behaving in specific ways to make ourselves good enough for divine acceptance, especially by doing more, more, more. If we pray more, serve more, give more, or add more charitable service to our overly crowded lives, we *might* make ourselves good enough. Thus, we become holy . . . in our own minds.

Instead of thinking of the Christian life as what we do, isn't it time to emphasize once again what God does? That's really the biblical perspective; Scripture provides hundreds of examples of the Holy breaking into human existence, chasing us, wooing us, reaching out toward us, embracing us, and changing us.

Let's think of the divine pursuit this way: For many Christians, the awareness begins when the Holy bursts into our lives and disrupts us, and we don't joyously welcome that disruption. Initially we resist, even though we know God wants only good for us.

Many times throughout the years, I've cried out to God (in my rebellious moods) and asked why I was the object of such a divine quest. I never heard a voice from heaven, but I have learned this much: I'm not unique. This "stalking" goes on in all our lives, because God has called each of us "according to his purpose. . . . For God knew his people in advance, and he chose them to become like his Son" (Romans 8:28–29 NLT).

As we become aware of this constant wooing from heaven, we also realize that we can't compare ourselves to others, because God doesn't speak to all of us with the same voice. The Pursuing One places a strict obedience upon us so that we can't measure our lives or compare ourselves to other believers. At times it seems as if some of the "good"

Christians—even the great leaders of the church—can do things that we're not allowed to do.

To make it worse, we find it difficult to talk about the Relentless Spirit that pursues us. If we do speak up, we assume others will call us proud for being so "humble," think us strange for having such off-center ideas, or raise an indifferent eyebrow to our naïveté.

For instance, long after I became a published writer, I found it hard to understand how other authors could push themselves into the public eye, unabashedly promote themselves and their books, and become famous for barely mediocre writing. "Oh, Lord, I know I'm a better writer," I moaned. (I'm not very objective about myself, so they may actually be better writers than I am.)

When I tried to follow their example, I felt such deep mortification that I despised my actions and backed away. I decided I'd rather sit in an obscure corner than receive applause that I had generated for myself.

I've heard others boast of their successes, especially of the copies their books have sold or of the large advance they received for their next one. I can't do that. I don't despise those who do, but I remind myself that One-Who-Loves-Me-and-Will-Not-Let-Me-Go has grabbed my hand and holds it firmly. When I try to pull away or to go out on my own, the divine fingers tighten their grip. Instead of singing to the world about my ability, my song is of the amazing grace that saved (and continues to save) a wretch like me.

I'm not trying to present myself as a humble, self-effacing

servant. What I am trying to make clear is that God just doesn't let up on us until the completion of the process of sanctification, which doesn't come in this life. The process differs in each of us; the result is the same.

God won't let me go. Even though I haven't always rejoiced in that fact, sometimes arguing and screaming, I'm thankful that God hasn't stopped the divine quest for me. I also know that as long as I live, God will relentlessly pursue me to complete sanctification.

This is true for each of us, and it means that if we pause and listen, we'll hear the divine whisper, the love call, the sweet promises, the tender voice that beckons us onward. It's the Unyielding Savior who accepts us as we are, yet never allows us to remain as we are.

That's the God I write about in this book—not only the Holy Chaser in my own life, but the one of so many relentless pursuits in the Bible.

CHAPTER ONE

ENCOUNTERING THE HOLY

I once read of a mythological creature called the basilisk. Born with the face of a lizard, it grew to an enormous size, perhaps as tall as twelve feet. Its body, similar to a rooster, represented sleepless vigilance. Three snakes, suggesting diabolical cunning, made up its six-foot-long tail. Despite having strong, pointed claws, it killed its victims—especially human beings—merely by breathing on them (they died of fright).

The legend goes on to say that the tormented human race found only one way to kill the horrible creature that ordinarily lived two hundred years. Whenever a basilisk charged, the community hurriedly elected one brave soul to run up to the beast and hold up something that reflected the basilisk's horrible image. When the monster gazed at its features mirrored back, it shuddered and died in horror.

As I've thought of this story, it's made me consider what it would be like if we faced the awesome God of the Bible. I suspect we might feel like dying merely from shame or from the realization of the pain we have caused our loving Savior. In addition to this, how would we react if God held the mirror up to us and we clearly gazed at ourselves?

Suppose the Divine Pursuer enabled us to see the hidden-to-us side of our personalities. Carl Jung invented a term called the "shadow side" to refer to our dark, unknown parts. I like to think of it as our backside—the parts of ourselves we can't see, don't want to see, or don't know exist.

Another way to say this is that God is "Utterly Other," as a seminary professor once said. The best word I can use to describe that otherness is *holy*. God is set apart, different, unlike the ordinary; that is, God is totally unlike human creatures.

For us to become the people of God's intended purpose, we have to change. We've all been infused with and tainted by sin; not one *part* of us is free from it. This sin, then, displeases God, the Wholly Other—the *Holy* Other. Not willing to leave us as we are, the seemingly Ruthless One chases us and never gives up.

In those moments of being caught by my divine pursuer, I've felt like the basilisk that sees its own reflection. On each occasion, God held a mirror to my face and forced me to gaze at my reflection. I detested the sight of myself. Facing that horrid image so revolted me that I cried out for help. These experiences became divine agents of change to push me forward in my growth. It was as if God smiled, embraced me, held me tightly, and whispered, "Gotcha."

Oༀ

I want to share an overwhelming incident where the Pursuing God caught me off guard, made me gaze deeply at myself, and refused to let me deny what I saw. Although it happened a long time ago, I can still vividly recall the traumatic experience of seeing myself.

At the time, I had served a little more than two years in Kenya as a missionary. The events leading up to that moment don't sound like anything horrible; it wasn't the event itself but the painful view the Holy One gave me of myself through that occasion.

The incident began when two African Christian leaders asked about an American woman named Evelyn (not her real name) who was coming to Nyanza province to work. She was to live with other missionaries about an hour's drive away.

Curious about her, one of them asked, "Does she have a husband and children?"

"No, she's divorced," I replied. "Her two sons are staying in the United States to finish their education." After all, the information wasn't a secret, so I never thought anything about giving them an honest and open answer.

Shortly after Evelyn arrived, one of the African pastors said something about her being divorced. When she learned that I had told someone who in turn had told him, her anger flared.

The next day Evelyn confronted me with these words: "You had no right to tell anyone that I'm divorced!" For perhaps ten minutes she called me insensitive, irresponsible, and a gossipmonger. No matter how much I tried to protest ignorance of her sensitivity, she continued to lash out.

"I'm sorry," I said, meaning it. "How was I to know?"

Her words screamed at me again: "If you had any feelings whatsoever, you'd know better!"

"I'm sorry," I stammered again.

Eventually, she walked away, jumped in her Land Rover, and drove off.

She had been extremely harsh, and on any other occasion I would have decided that she had grossly overreacted. Yet as I watched the red dust billow behind her vehicle, I couldn't shrug off her accusation. Something happened to me as I stood on the concrete front porch. Tears filled my eyes. "I'm sorry," I mumbled. Then I asked God to forgive me. Yet instead of finding instant relief, I only felt worse.

Looking back, the trigger to the event seems rather trivial, yet the effects were anything but. Long after I could no longer hear the engine or see the dust, I faced being captured by my loving and unrelenting Savior.

I felt as if the All-Seeing Eyes of heaven had bored into my soul. I saw myself as I really was, and I hated what I saw. I felt like Job when he groaned, "I loathe my life" (9:21). Never before had I felt such revulsion toward myself. I faced the impurity of my motives, the evil that lurked inside me, and I recoiled at my callousness toward other people.

Granted, Evelyn had been overly sensitive and had reacted more angrily than the situation deserved. As I learned later, she herself was a gossip and epitomized most of the things of which she accused me. It may have been a case of what therapists call displaced anger; that is, she may have yelled at me instead of screaming at herself. Anyway, that part hardly matters.

Evelyn spoke enough truth in her accusations that the Holy Other nudged me and made me stare at my gross reflection. The Pursuing Spirit had used Evelyn to hold up a mirror and force me to face who I was. The sight horrified me; tears filled my eyes, and I was hardly able to accept how powerfully her anger was affecting me.

Finally, I walked into the house and went straight into my room. I dropped onto the bed, filled with remorse and deep frustration. The anger soon gave way to depression, an emotion I had never experienced before. I'd had down moments like everyone else, but nothing like this. I had harmed someone: *That's the way you are, and you hurt people all the time,* whispered a voice inside my head.

It was true.

I hated what I heard.

What must I have looked like to the Holy One in my utter, total sinfulness? Shame overpowered me, and I felt as if everyone knew all the secret sins of my soul. Or, if they didn't already know, if they looked at me, I felt as if my evil would be painted on my face for all to condemn.

For the next three days, I hardly left the house. I asked

my wife to answer the door and explain to people that I wasn't feeling well.

※

In telling this, I want to make it clear that I was a believer when this incident took place. I was a born-again Christian, a disciple, a follower, or whatever term anyone wanted to use. For almost nine years I had zealously served my Savior.

When I initially turned to Jesus Christ, I acknowledged my sinfulness and knew I had many things wrong with me. Mostly, however, I saw God as a loving and compassionate Father who welcomed me as a beloved child. The real sin issue didn't hit me for nine years.

For three days after Evelyn's anger flashed on me, I read and reread Romans, especially the plaintive cry of Paul in chapter 7, where he acknowledges his sinfulness. I truly understood it for the first time. *This is a portrait of me,* I thought. *This is where I am right now. I know the good and the right, but I don't seem able to obey.* Before this experience, I had been taught that when Paul wrote Romans 7:14–25, he was reflecting on his own pre-conversion days.

As I memorized most of those verses, I knew they were not the inner conflicts of a new convert. This agony could only have come from the mature Paul—the man who sought God (or had been sought by God), endured all the hardships and threats that his enemies could throw at him, and still stood firm in his faith. Somewhere in his life, when he wrote these words, Paul felt like a basilisk, abhorring what he saw. He viewed himself as never before and recoiled from the image.

❧

Writing now, years after my experience in Africa, I still reflect on the day I peered into the face of the Holy. The Spirit showed me myself, and I couldn't stand to gaze into those eyes. "How can you possibly love me?" I cried out. "How can you accept me—evil, sinful person that I am?"

In addition to hardly leaving the house, I barely slept during the three nights following my experience with Evelyn. A few times I went outside and walked in the darkness. The muted cries of animals or glimpses of someone carrying a lantern on Giribe Mountain momentarily diverted me. Each time I'd hear myself wail, "Is there no forgiveness, no hope for me?"

As I gradually pulled out of my despair, the one comforting thought was this: *God has known everything about me all along and has continued to love me.*

Almost a week later I was up before dawn, walking around the compound. Just before six o'clock the first rays of light sneaked across the horizon, and I watched in awe as the sun brought new light into the world. "Thank you, God," I said softly. Then I became aware that the despair and sadness had gone, and joyful praise emerged. God not only knew everything but also cared enough to confront me with the truth about myself.

Could we stand the sight of our unknown self, shown to

us by the Holy? In fact, I think that's one of the reasons for the relentless pursuit of our loving Savior. When we see our naked image and the sight horrifies us, we're ready to plead, "Help! Change me!"

I've caught a glimpse—and I'm glad it was only a glimpse—of myself. I've seen parts of me that I didn't like. In my revulsion, I heard myself say aloud, "I can't stand the sight. Please, please deliver me." On reflection—and that reflection came a long time afterward—I can now admit that the encounter became one of those sacred moments where the Holy showed me how unholy I am. God had caught up with me, and I couldn't run away.

As I ponder the idea of the Holy chasing us, I recognize that while we mature in our faith—and as part of that ruthless demand for our sanctification—God reveals our inner selves to us, slowly and patiently illuminating things we haven't wanted to know about who we are. If we face the dark side of ourselves, we won't die of fright like with the basilisk, but as one friend said, "We *feel* like dying."

We also need to remind ourselves that the Pursuer shows us only as much as we can handle at one time. Graciously, the Holy One withholds the worst parts of us from our sight until we can survive the encounter. Or, as I think of it, until the Holy Chaser outruns us again.

We modern Christians aren't alone. Since the beginning of the human race, the Holy has chased after us. Individuals react differently—some recoil in horror, some run from what they see and never stop until they die, and others beg God to take away the emblazoned image before their eyes. At times, I've successfully denied what I saw or minimized its importance.

In my own case, these escapes are only temporary. God chases me like a hound of heaven, to use the metaphor of Francis Thompson. The Hunter chases me down every highway, byway, and detour until I reach the sign that reads, "Dead End." Then I'm caught and forced to surrender. I've resisted because I knew it would cause me agony and inner groaning, and I'd have to see darkness inside myself. But eventually I see the results—that's what makes the surrender worthwhile. When God finishes that particular pursuit, I don't hear, "Go, and sin no more." Instead, I feel a firm arm on my shoulder, with a gentle voice that says, "I am with you always."

I've never found any instance in the Bible of a divine encounter that brings immediate joy (although see chapter 10, the story of Samuel). Praise and thanksgiving do come—later. At the *moment* of confrontation, when the Holy intervenes, we're faced with ourselves: a hideous sight that alarms, terrifies, and haunts us. We focus on ourselves because that's all we can see reflected in the mirror before our eyes.

Looking back, I also realize that being chased and caught by the Holy is a necessary step on the way to spiritual maturity. We can grow when God whispers a word of wisdom, or when we receive insight so that we know exactly how to handle a situation. We're in desperate financial straits, unable to

pay the mortgage, and then the money arrives from an unexpected source. Doctors insist that my child has no chance to
survive, and then she miraculously recovers. In such moments,
we're filled with joy and our commitment deepens.

The most powerful spurts of growth, however, come after
we've gazed into the mirror of reality. The Spirit holds up a
passage from the Bible, sends a servant to confront us, or
speaks directly to us in a moment of receptivity—we stare at
our shadow side. In such moments, like the great apostle, we
cry out, "I do not understand my own actions. For I do not do
what I want, but I do the very thing I hate. . . . Wretched man
that I am! Who will rescue me from this body of death?"
(Romans 7:15, 24).

If we face the awful sight of our shadow side and allow
God to guide us through the anguish, we move onward and
reach the place where, like Paul, we rejoice: "Thanks be to
God through Jesus Christ our Lord!" (7:25). Yet not everyone
makes the transition from verse 24 to verse 25. Some never
get past the agony, the pain, of the horrid self-portrait. Others
stay immobilized for long periods. I've come to realize that
the pain doesn't precede the cure—the pain is part of the healing. We can't fix what we can't face.

One of my e-mail friends sent me this quote from Carl
Rogers: "The curious paradox is that when I accept myself just
as I am, then I can change." The Holy can work in us only
when we stare at our horrid image and cry out, "That's *my* face
I see!" God can then either remove the offensive sight or enable us to cope with it. Sometimes we have the sense that

we've moved three giant steps toward overcoming, but we know the battle isn't over yet.

My African experience, when the Holy One caught me, changed the course of my life. Even though it didn't transform me into instant sainthood, it did bring to me an awareness of my shadow side and an appreciation that God was carefully and slowly removing those displeasing elements of my being.

I had encountered the seemingly Ruthless God who loves me enough to pursue me until I surrendered. The ordeal had hurt, and even now, years later, I can still feel the sting of that experience.

But it has been worth the pain.

CHAPTER TWO

THE REVERSED QUESTION

W here are you?"
This is an important question to think about. It's especially significant to contemplate the first time it appears in human history. God directs the question to Adam, to force the man to gaze deeply at himself and to see what God already knew.

The occasion takes place in the Garden of Eden. After providing abundantly for all human needs, God gave the man and the woman one negative command: They were not to eat of the tree of the knowledge of good and evil (see Genesis 2:16–17). They disobeyed.

What God understood, and what the couple couldn't possibly understand before their failure to obey, was that they knew only the good and had no understanding of evil. After they ate, they grasped the meaning of evil as well. That knowledge would banish their power to opt for the good.

They became sinners, and their perfect world crashed.

The Creator had promised that by their disobedience they would know evil—and now they did. In realizing what evil was, they had no power to help themselves. They were trapped with their knowledge of the facts and their inability to do anything to extricate themselves.

From that time on, the Bible declares that all human beings are sinners from the moment of birth. Most of us Christians have no trouble acknowledging this. Where we hesitate is to admit that innate human sin always guides us to choose evil. We can soften this and say we're self-centered or concerned more about our needs than anything else, but the fact that we don't like admitting the thoroughness of our sinful nature is part of the sinful condition itself! The Bible reveals the truth: *Aside from the grace of God*, we'll always opt for the most self-centered solution.

Here are a few verses (paraphrased) that speak of the human condition:

- "We have all gone astray and are perverse" (Psalm 14:3a).
- "None of us does good—not one of us" (Psalm 14:3b).
- "No one is righteous or seeks God" (Romans 3:10–11).
- "We have turned aside, become worthless, and don't know how to show kindness" (Romans 3:12).
- "Our mouths are open graves [or perhaps we'd say 'sewers' today], and we deceive with our tongues" (Romans 3:13).

Other places in the Bible make the same point and conclude that the reward for following our self-centered way is death, but God's gift through Jesus Christ is life eternal. (See Romans 6:23.)

❦

In stark language, the Bible gives us the result of Adam and Eve's disobedience: "Then the eyes of both were opened, and they knew that they were naked" (Genesis 3:7a). This statement doesn't portray God holding the mirror to their eyes—at least not quite—but the action has begun because of their failure.

Their disobedience results in a sudden realization: *They were naked*. Had they been naked all along? Apparently so, but now the awareness of their condition flooded their mind, and shame covered them. Why else would they take the next step—the covering up of their bodies? "They sewed fig leaves together and made loincloths for themselves" (Genesis 3:7b).

They were afraid and they were ashamed, so they tried to hide from themselves the awful awareness of their new sinful condition. They feared, although the Bible doesn't mention the object of the fear, so I can only assume they feared that God would punish them. Now that their minds had embraced sin and evil, fear, worry, and anxiety surely marched in as well. Certainly when we realize we've done wrong, fear of punishment scores rather high.

That's the first thing we learn about Adam and Eve's reaction to the forbidden fruit. It's not only the loss of their innocence, but it's also the destruction of trust—reliance on their

Creator. They had not been in need of clothing or anything else because God had provided for them; now they make the first moves toward independence from God. Until that moment, they had relied totally on divine provisions, but now they knew things would be different—they knew they were sinners. Would God's wrath destroy them? Would the Divine Provider no longer feed them? Would they enter into a sleep that didn't end?

Their Creator had threatened them with death. Although in their state of innocence they probably had no understanding of the term, they must have feared that they would no longer exist. Perhaps a better way to read the meaning of God's threat and its enactment is to think that at the moment of disobedience something died within them. Physical death would come later.

But there's more. When innocence died, something took its place. One name we can give this is "conscience." The function of conscience is to point us only one way—toward guilt and negativity, to make us aware of *not* doing the right thing. Isn't it interesting that conscience is conspicuously quiet when we make the right choices?

One act of disobedience shattered the lives of Adam and Eve. They could experience guilt, shame, remorse, pain, or regret, but they could never again feel innocent, whole, clean, or guiltless. They had dirtied their souls, and they knew the reality without any means of making themselves better or repairing the damage. We have inherited the same dilemma.

The early chapters of Genesis lay out a powerful truth—The All-Powerful One created humanity perfect. That is, God created the human race in the *divine image* (Genesis 1:27). We don't know precisely what that term means, but we do know that the original pair was perfect until something, sometime, and someplace changed them to imperfect. So we need to ask: What does God want us to understand not only about the man and his wife in the Garden but also about ourselves and about all humanity? What made them—and their descendants—want to hide from God? Why did they *need* to hide?

The story doesn't end with their being naked and afraid; it leads to the first human pursuit by the Holy. The Bible reads simply: "They heard the sound of the LORD God walking in the garden at the time of the evening breeze, and the man and his wife hid themselves from the presence of the LORD God among the trees of the garden" (Genesis 3:8).

"Where are you?" God asked the man (3:9).

The action by the couple becomes the prototype of human experience as they attempt to hide themselves from God. Obviously, there is no literal way they could do this. There is, however, a method we have learned by being the offspring of Adam and Eve: We call it denial or self-deception. Denial means looking at our naked souls and saying, "I'm not naked." Self-deception refuses to see the reality of our own selves—and we all have the innate capacity to do it exceedingly well.

Instead of showing mercy, offering forgiveness, or meting out justice, God asks a second question, "Who told you that you were naked?" (3:11a), and follows it with a third: "Have you eaten from the tree of which I commanded you not to eat?" (3:11b).

Adam set the standard for the rest of us—self-justification and blame—by pointing to his wife and saying, "Uh, well, God, it was like this. This wife *you* gave me—she's the one who did it. She disobeyed and then gave me some of the fruit, and, you know, to please her, I took a few bites" (my version of Genesis 3:12).

The relentlessness of God pushes on, and the fourth question, this time to Eve, becomes: "What is this that you have done?" (3:13).

Eve's no different from Adam, because she points her finger at the Tempter and says, "He made me do it" (3:13, paraphrased).

Isn't this how we respond when the Holy Pursuer catches up with us? We begin by denying the truth or refusing to face the reality. We blame people, circumstances, and childhood experiences—anything other than ourselves. We do anything we can to avoid seeing ourselves as we are or facing our despicable actions against God.

Even to say that we learned it from Adam sounds as if we're doing the same thing the first couple did. That's not my intention in writing this, but each of us, in some form, is like the enlightened Adam and Eve. The knowledge of the wrong we have done flashes upon our consciousness. If we face the reality, we call it sin. Or we minimize our actions and call them mistakes or misunderstandings, or we play the blame game: "If she hadn't said that to me, I wouldn't have . . ." "If only you had . . ."

For the Holy One to pursue and catch us means to encounter ourselves. Yet it's more. If we see only ourselves, we end up in despair and hopelessness. If we also see God holding up a mirror to our eyes, then we can ask for help in our despair.

Seeing the divine hand holding the mirror tells us God is saying, "I want you to see your action for what it is—a deliberate act of disobedience." The hand on the mirror also says, "I have chosen to show you this to make you realize that I am offering help."

Let's look at those questions again:

- "Where are you?"
- "Who told you that you were naked?"
- "Have you disobeyed my command?"
- "What is this that you have done?"

Four questions, but they aren't idle ones. If we answer them, resist running away, or refuse to try to hide from the truth, we see the road of forgiveness laid out for us. The answer to the first question, "Where are you?" is simply, "I'm right here, Lord. Right here in my sinful, faithless actions."

"Who told you that you were naked?" Because God endowed us with a sense of self-awareness, part of its function is to enable us to accept our failures and weaknesses. At its best, this also points to the Divine Pursuer. Our sense of what's right and wrong, we're told, comes from being taught. So the second answer can be, "I knew it was wrong" or "Your Holy Spirit spoke to me."

The third question, "Have you disobeyed my command?" has only one honorable answer: "Yes."

Finally, the fourth question asks what we have done, and the answer is, "I have disobeyed" or "I have broken your holy laws" or "I have failed" or "I have sinned."

The point of the questions, just as when originally asked, is to force us to gaze deeply within and to see our nakedness and, hence, our sinfulness. Only as we give the proper answers to God *and ourselves* can we move on. Only after we know the curse of the disease do we find the healing balm.

In the beginning, the Creator came to the couple in the Garden and asked, "Where are you?" Today, something has happened to that question. Instead of allowing God to speak, we reverse the situation and cry out, "God, where are you?"

I suspect this is one of the reasons we have so much spiritual trouble: we're demanding answers from God. Our lives have hit a snare, or everything seemingly goes wrong, and we start by calling God into account. Sometimes it's simply "Why me?" or "What did I do to deserve this?" When we ask, "Where are you?" isn't it really a demand, or a petulant cry, or at least a wail of frustration? We expect God to answer and to show the divine presence, and we get upset when God doesn't say, "Here I am."

Isn't it possible that the Divine Pursuer rightfully insists that we answer instead of ask? Could it be that our loving Creator is using the same method on us that we find was used with Adam? Maybe the way to approach the question when bleak days overshadow our lives is to ask, "Where *am I*, God?"

In the case of the first couple, they deliberately disobeyed. Our actions may not be quite as overtly evil, but we don't know until we've engaged in some amount of self-scrutiny. "Where am I?" If we begin by looking inward, we might be able to look upward and see the smiling face of God and hear the voice reply, "Ah, now you have it."

What would have happened if Adam had answered, "I'm here, Lord, because I'm ashamed. I disobeyed you"? What would happen if we said, "Here I am, God. Help me search my heart"?

God asks, relentlessly it seems. In fact, I suspect that's why we constantly have the penetrating question thrown at us. If we listen and hear the divine intention—and it takes courage for us to do this—we're a lot farther down the yellow brick road toward heaven than if we insist on being the asker. Could it be that God asks us so that we're forced to look at ourselves? Isn't it a distinct possibility that God wants us to say, "I'm naked, and I hid from you"?

Instead, we try to beat God by starting and (we think) controlling the conversation. If we call the Holy One into question for lack of action on our behalf, we keep the spotlight off ourselves. Slick work. I wonder if this isn't the modern version of sewing fig leaves to hide nakedness.

This, then, leads me to point out that being confronted by the Holy comes with divine intentionality. This is the on-going, unrelenting pursuit for our good and to accomplish our sanctification. In its simplest form, it is to bring us into such sharp accountability that in all ways we become more like Jesus Christ.

Perhaps the psalmist said it best for us: "Search me, O God, and know my heart; test me and know my thoughts. See if there is any wicked way in me, and lead me in the way everlasting" (139:23–24).

When we sincerely pray in this vein, we know that our Savior is embracing us. The pursuit has ended—temporarily, of course, because we soon insist on breaking away. And when we face the cold and darkness of life, we tend to cry out, "Where are you, God?"

Some of us, however, are learning to go back to the original intent of the question: "God, where am I?"

For those of us who sense the divine pursuit, there is an answer: "I am in your hand."

CHAPTER THREE

AN IMPOSSIBLE SACRIFICE

I've done everything you've asked. Without arguing, I left my homeland and my friends. I've been faithful. You made promises to me, and I believed them. You promised me a son, the one thing both Sarah and I wanted. For twenty-five years we waited and prayed every day, and then, when I was a hundred years old, blessed God that you are, you gave us that son, and it was a miracle, because we were too old to have children."

Maybe that's when tears slipped down ancient Abraham's cheeks. As he stares at the sleeping form of his young son, Isaac, he's not just a follower of the True God of Heaven. He's also the father of a young boy—and God apparently wants to take away that son for whom the old man had waited so many years, and then Abraham would be childless again.

The command doesn't make sense. How could God give Abraham a son and then a few years later ask him to sacrifice the boy on an altar? He would have to personally kill the child before he burned his body as a sacrifice. "Is that what I must do to prove my faithfulness to you? Surely, you can't require this of me."

Earlier testings had been difficult, but there is something more than paternal grief and anguish brought about by the impending death of Abraham's only son. It would have been sad for him to be deprived of Isaac, yet sadder still that this son should die by a violent death; the worst part being that Abraham himself has been appointed as executioner.

The old man might not have thought about it at the moment because of his personal grief, but there is another significant factor here. God commands him to slay his only son, the one who will provide heirs so that his offspring will become as many as the sands of the seashore. With the pending loss of his son, the salvation of the world would seem to be extinguished; the God who promised to bring light into the world through Isaac said, "It is through Isaac that offspring shall be named for you" (Genesis 21:12).

How can Abraham be faithful and godly at the same time? Surely the grieving father must have asked that question. The death of the boy would have been the destruction of faith. Everything would come to a despicable end. How could such a thing be?

At this moment we see the nature of the divine testing. It's difficult and painful to Abraham to forget that he's the boy's father, and he needs to push away all human affections to obey God. It must have been more difficult to endure the disgrace of shameful cruelty by becoming the executioner of his own son.

꩜

"Sacrifice your son."

What an odious command. What turmoil Abraham must have suffered. My assumption is that he argued with God. I would have. Either he would have said, "This can't be God speaking" or "This is too much to ask." I assume it was the latter.

"What more can I have to do with you, God, when the only pledge of your grace is now being taken away?" By calling Isaac Abraham's *only* son, God irritates the wound inflicted by the banishment of the older son, Ishmael, who was not acknowledged by God, at least not acknowledged as an heir or as a promised son.

As Abraham struggles, surely he remembers his older son, Ishmael, who is now lost to him. Although his son, Ishmael was not born to Sarah but to Hagar, his wife's servant. For a slave to become the surrogate mother for a barren woman wasn't such an unusual thing in that primitive culture. Hagar was Sarah's property, and so the child sired by Abraham with the slave would have been hers as well. She said to her husband, "You see that the LORD has prevented me from bearing children; go in to my slave-girl; it may be that I shall obtain children by her" (Genesis 16:2).

Abraham did as Sarah asked. "When [Hagar] saw that she

[was pregnant], she looked with contempt on her mistress" (16:4). We don't know details, but we assume the slave taunted Sarah, which would have been easy enough to do. If a woman couldn't bear a child, she was considered cursed.

Sarah not only feels abandoned and cursed by God but her own servant despises her. After the birth of her own son, she begs Abraham, "Cast out this slave woman with her son; for the son of this slave woman shall not inherit along with my son Isaac" (21:10).

To cast out Ishmael must have thrown Abraham into a painful state. This was *his* son—his own firstborn male, the dream of every ancient man. Here is all the Bible says: "The matter was very distressing to Abraham on account of his son. But God said to Abraham, 'Do not be distressed because of the boy ... for it is through Isaac that offspring shall be named for you'" (21:12). God further promised to make Ishmael into a great nation, but it wouldn't be the chosen people.

For most of us, *distressed* would mean grief, anguish, regret, sorrow, perhaps despair, even depression. Common sense says that Abraham must have pleaded with God to find another way instead of disowning his son—which is what casting him away surely had to be.

We don't know for certain how old Ishmael was at the time his father sent him away. Genesis 16:16 states that Abraham was eighty-six when Ishmael was born, which would have him fourteen years older than Isaac. We also know that Abraham held a feast for Isaac after he was weaned. Normally mothers weaned their children between the ages of two and four.

Ishmael was probably about sixteen. That meant that he was likely considered a man. He might have lost his inheritance as the older, firstborn son, but he wasn't a three-year-old sent away to die.

Regardless of his age, it couldn't have been easy for Abraham to turn his back on his own child. But despite his personal pain, Abraham sent Ishmael and Hagar away. The implication is that they never saw each other again. I find that extremely hard to grasp. Even as I try to write about it, and despite making allowances for a different culture and a more primitive society, it just doesn't make sense to me. Never to see his own son again had to have been a heavy burden for Abraham to bear. In fact, wasn't this an immense test? His consolation was that he did have a son, the one God had promised, the one Sarah bore to him when she was ninety and Abraham was one hundred.

Now as the boy Isaac grew, his parents probably indulged him in every way—maybe too much, so that the boy became the center of their lives. We don't know the extent of their doting, but we do know what God told Abraham, "Take your son, your only son Isaac, whom you love, and go to the land of Moriah, and offer him there as a burnt offering on one of the mountains that I shall show you" (Genesis 22:2). The Bible records this incident factually, with little emotion.

Although the biblical record gives no details, it seems clear that Abraham didn't doubt the command as coming from God. Surely the aged patriarch knew the divine voice. For him to know the will of God wasn't the issue; the dilemma centers on carrying it out. This man had known testing, temptation, and years of waiting for the fulfillment of the promises. He received a command, one that wounded him more than if Isaac had died in an accident or by illness.

The next verse (22:3) reads, "So Abraham rose early in the morning, saddled his donkey, and took two of his young men with him, and his son Isaac; he cut the wood for the burnt offering, and set out and went to the place in the distance that God had shown him." He had done everything to prepare for the sacrifice of his son. Now he only had to follow through.

"But I can't," the old man must have insisted. "This is an impossible sacrifice. Please, don't make me do it." At some point he must have argued the logic of this command: "How can you do this to me? You want to take Isaac? After I waited for him for twenty-five years? How can you ask this?"

We don't know what words the aged man used or how much anguish he suffered. We have only the straight narrative in Genesis that contains God's command and Abraham's obedience. This may be one of those poignant stories where silence speaks more powerfully than words. Surely the original hearers must have felt the shock, the outrage, and the pain of that father.

Behind the whole story, of course, is God's purpose. The story begins with an editorial comment: "God tested Abraham" (22:1). Here's my sense of this experience: God knew Abraham's heart and that the man doted on his boy. Certainly that was understandable. After all, for anyone at that age to have a son, and especially to have waited a quarter of a century for the fulfillment of the promise, why wouldn't he?

Yet I find something repugnant about Abraham's taking Isaac to Mount Moriah to kill him. As a parent—even as a human being—to think of taking the life of a child is more than I could handle.

Abraham lived in a different time and culture. Fathers had total control over their children's lives. Pagan parents *did* offer their children to their gods. Abraham's action may not have been so repulsive in his era. For some, his obedience may have expressed a form of mystical allegiance and commitment. In other societies, it was always the firstborn son the father sacrificed, the assumption being that they would have other children to replace him.

Except in this case there seemed to be no possibility that Abraham and Sarah would have another child, let alone a boy.

Years earlier, Abraham had to part company from his nephew Lot because their herds were too large to graze together; they went separate ways. We can easily assume that Lot had been like a son to the childless man.

Lot was gone.

Ishmael had been sent away.

Now Abraham must offer Isaac as a sacrifice.

It's easy for us as readers to rush past this painful episode, because we know the purpose behind the incident. We also know the end of the story. This wasn't true for Abraham.

&

After three days of traveling to the mountains, Abraham saw the place. He left his workers behind and went the rest of the journey with only Isaac. "Abraham took the wood of the burnt offering and laid it on his son Isaac, and he himself carried the fire and the knife" (22:6). The sacrifice is ready, but now God speaks again: "Do not lay your hand on the boy or do anything to him; for now I know that you fear God, since you have not withheld your son, your only son, from me" (22:12).

We have the framework of the story from the beginning: God did this as the last great test for Abraham. We also have the ending—God stopped the killing and commended the patriarch for his faithful obedience.

After all, God had promised a son, and had made it clear that Isaac was the one promised. The promise, however, involved more than having a male offspring: As mentioned, the boy was to be the receiver of the great covenant to have as many children as the sands of the seashore. He was to be the one who would perpetuate the line of the faithful (21:12). What happens when the *command* of God conflicts with the *promise* of God? Certainly, Abraham wouldn't have shrugged and said, "Okay, then."

&

As I've pondered this story, I've discovered that it may be obvious what is going on. Isaac had become an idol—something that took the old man's eyes off of God. This was a command to force Abraham to look deep inside himself.

This is the divine pursuit, or what I like to call an invasion of the Holy. This interruption makes us face our desires and our motives. When the Holy chases us and forces us to look inward, we feel distress and pain. We lose our comfortable foundations and—at least momentarily—nothing in life holds any meaning.

God stares into our eyes, and it confuses us, hurts us, maybe even angers or terrifies us. We turn away, unwilling to face what the Holy shows us: "You have another god!" I can hear the divine voice saying, "You have put so much of your affection elsewhere that it diminishes your affection and commitment to me." Only God knows the real desires within us. Only the Sovereign Creator of the world can slip beyond the words *behavior* and *masks* and make us stare into God's holy, scrutinizing eyes.

"You have a choice. You must choose."

I doubt that Abraham consciously put his boy before his love for God. My assumption is that the old man praised the Lord for the miracle when it finally took place. In the days that followed, his love for the infant grew. Somewhere that love crossed the line, and his son became number one in his life.

Now the trial has value. Why would God order him to slay the boy if it wasn't the most difficult ordeal possible? Isn't that the purpose of a divine test? The response of God at the end helps us see this: "Now I know that you fear God, since you have not withheld your son" (22:12).

Isn't it also possible that Abraham struggled from more than the loss of his son? Could it also be that he was being forced to choose between God's command, which made no sense to him, and the person of God? Could it also be that the lure of the promises and the fulfillment through Isaac had taken the man's eyes off the Giver of all good things?

In some ways it seems strange to look at Abraham as one of those individuals whom God pursued. He's the father of the faithful, both in the Old Testament and the New. Today even Muslims look to Father Abraham through Ishmael.

Why this test? Why did the Holy pursue at exactly this point in the man's life? For this we find only one answer. The only way Abraham—or any of us—moves fully in the right direction is that the Holy breaks into our lives and lovingly points out that we're moving in the wrong direction. This is one way the divine pursuit works. When God's interruption occurred, Abraham saw himself. He was unclean, imperfect, and an idol worshiper.

This test came because it was exactly where the aged follower of God most needed the divine finger to point. This was his one place of resistance. For years the old man had prayed and waited for God's fulfilled promise. Isn't it easy to see that once he received his heart's desire, the desire took over his heart? Isn't it obvious that the object of God's faithfulness had become the object to replace God?

This was exactly where God needed to invade and pursue. This was exactly what Abraham needed to face: whether his long-desired gift was more important than the will of God. Few of us will have such invasions of the Holy. Maybe this is because the impediments to following God are too many and too large to allow us to attain such a spiritual level.

Maybe there are too many little things in our lives God has to confront. If so, think of the purity of Abraham's faith: the Holy had reached the core of his desires. It wasn't only "Give me your son"; the command was stronger. God asked for his son—his only son—*whom you love*" (Genesis 22:2). This made Abraham stare into God's holy mirror. It wasn't that he merely loved the boy, but that maybe he loved him too much.

That's where the unrelenting pursuit by the Holy comes in. It's not just love, but love that goes beyond the boundaries—love that moves into adoration—love that usurps the place in our heart intended only for God.

The best illustration I can give of a contemporary version is from my own marriage. Shirley and I had been married about a year before she said, "Something is wrong. When I pray, I have this image of a great wall between God and me." We talked about it and prayed together. Eventually she said to me, "You're the wall. I've put you before God."

An acknowledgment, confession, and a renewed commitment to God was all it took. Those who knew Shirley wouldn't have guessed this to be true of her. As her husband,

I saw a consistent, committed relationship to Jesus Christ. Shirley knew, even though no one else could see it.

Is it possible that God may be expressing the deepest kindness and love to us when that voice says, "Slay your son"? "You shall have no other gods before me"?

I've given a lot of space in this chapter to trying to understand the pain and torment Abraham must have gone through, because too often we miss the humanness of biblical heroes. We often act as if when God speaks, the person jumps up and hurriedly obeys without question. I doubt Abraham could have done that. He loved his son.

In fact, that's why the story is so powerful. God's finger pointed to the great realm of weakness in the patriarch's life— the love for his long-awaited son. It's that testing, that demand, that makes for this powerful encounter of the Holy. In such moments of anguish, we face the fact that God has been pursuing us, often for a long time, and has finally grabbed us, saying lovingly, "Listen!"

I want to give one more illustration that relates to our text. It is the story of a friend whom I'll call Patrick. He used to speak often to me of his deep commitment to the Lord. When he'd start talking about his relationship to God, he'd say, "God is the most important part of my life. My wife, my family, no one and nothing comes even close." I don't think this was idle talk or spiritual boasting. His life consistently bore that out.

One day we were talking together in front of his house, when a speeding car struck his daughter. For the next ten hours we didn't know if she would live or not. During those hours of uncertainty, I caught a glimpse of my friend's heart. He cried and he anguished. At one point his personal pain was so great he became almost incoherent. With my arm around his shoulder, we walked down to the hospital chapel. I waited outside because I knew this was something he had to face alone.

Even where I stood and waited, I could hear Patrick's screams and his denunciations of God. He used harsh, accusing words I would never have expected to fall from his lips. This was a man in deepest despair.

I believe it was also a man who was being pursued by the Holy.

For a long time, maybe an hour, he agonized. When he finally came out, Patrick looked like a broken man. In the most humbled voice I'd ever heard from him, he said, "I've surrendered her to God."

I hugged him, being at a total loss for words. Later I wondered if *surrender* was the word the Holy had waited for.

Just before midnight, we got word that his daughter would recover. "The crisis has passed," the nurse assured us.

Yes, indeed, the crisis had passed. My friend had been pursued and caught. I saw him a lot over the next three or four years, until he moved away. Never again did he tell me how much he loved God. He didn't need to.

Now I knew, and I suspect others did as well. Patrick was

as committed to following God as any person I've ever known, and his actions reflected what his words no longer spoke.

His idol had been ripped away.

The Holy had encountered him.

And the Holy had changed him.

That's the purpose of the unrelenting pursuit of our lives.

CHAPTER FOUR

STRANGE REWARDS AND SUICIDAL COURAGE

No matter how beautifully the story reads, it still troubles me. The first time I read it as a new Christian, I could hardly believe it. The man had deceived his father, stolen the inheritance rightly belonging to his older brother, and before his father's death, he sneaked out of the country because he feared his defrauded brother, who had threatened to kill him.

That man, Jacob, runs away, heading for the homestead of his mother's people. On the journey, he spends the night in a field and uses a stone for a pillow. He has a magnificent dream, one to which Jesus makes reference in John 1:51. It's an odd event all the way through; in that vision, God appears to Jacob and promises unlimited blessings.

How can this be? Promises of good for doing wrong? Strange reward!

The account in Genesis 28 repeats the traditional covenant

given first to Abraham and later to Isaac. Now the fugitive Jacob, Abraham's grandson, hears those promises for himself. The land on which he lies sleeping will belong to him and to his descendants. The covenant also assures him that those descendants will be as numerous as "the dust of the earth" (28:14). Through Jacob—the deceiver and thief—and through his offspring, blessing will come to all.

This isn't everything. Although Jacob leaves the land, he is assured that the divine presence will be with him constantly. God won't forsake him and he will return to the land; he'll receive everything foretold to his father and grandfather.

Where's the rebuke? Where's the threat of punishment? Not one word. Instead, we read only promises of blessedness! God appears to bolster Jacob's flagging ego and confirms to him an inheritance he must have believed he had lost. God assures the corrupt man of divine aid in gaining everything as Isaac's heir.

Some preachers have tried to impress on us that after this momentous dream, Jacob changed. Really? If he did, there's no outward evidence of his rehabilitation. He doesn't stop scheming or doing underhanded tricks. For the next twenty years he cheats his father-in-law at every opportunity. The chapters after Genesis 28 recount one unholy deed after another by the scheming Jacob.

Despite his ongoing failures, remarkably Jacob does acknowledge God. After his dream at a place called Bethel, he breathlessly exclaims, "Surely the LORD is in this place—and I did not know it! . . . How awesome is this place! This is none other than the house of God, and this is the gate of heaven" (28:16–17).

Although they're wonderful words that seem to signify deep spiritual commitment, again, this man's behavior undergoes no transformation. It will take twenty years before the Divine Pursuer breaks through to Jacob, and at a time when he once again fears for his life.

To make the event at Bethel even more significant and the reward sound even more strange, the Bible records Jacob's responses to the wonderful promises: He bargains with the God of heaven. In fact, if anything, this increases the man's arrogance. God is with him, and he doesn't have to confess, change, repent, or go back home. The implication is that God will bless the fugitive simply because he has been chosen: "Then Jacob made a vow, saying, 'If God will be with me, and will keep me in this way that I go, and will give me bread to eat and clothing to wear, so that I come again to my father's house in peace, then the LORD shall be my God' " (28:20–21).

For the first time, as far as we know, at Bethel God encounters Jacob and holds out promises of lavish blessings. The man, in essence, responds with "Okay, if you do all these things, then you'll be my God."

Because of this response, some refer to it as Jacob's conversion. It certainly isn't. Others have called it a confessional moment for Jacob. It's not that either. It is an account of a man meeting God, hearing comforting words, and accepting those promises without admitting his need to change or to respond in gratitude. It's a scene where divine grace is extended to a most unworthy man. This is important to emphasize, because grace means—always—that the recipient doesn't deserve it. It's an offer of love, protection, guidance, and acceptance in spite of actions and attitudes. However, Jacob doesn't graciously respond to grace.

The best we can say about this story, the full account of which occurs in Genesis 28:10–22, is that Jacob recognizes the dream as a powerful moment in his life. The stone he had used for a pillow becomes part of a memorial pillar, a marker of the unforgettable appearance of God.

This can't be understated: Even after such a moving experience, Jacob remains unchanged. For the next two decades the Bible records all his devious actions (matching those of Laban, who becomes his father-in-law). If this were the end of Jacob's story, it wouldn't make much sense that it's recorded in the Bible. The truth is that it's only the prelude to God's relentless persistence: The Pursuing One targets Jacob and refuses to let go.

Let's fast-forward twenty years. Jacob has lived in Paddan-aram in Mesopotamia, and he's made such a mess of his relationship with his father-in-law that he decides to go home. He isn't broken and returning like the prodigal son. He no longer exudes that strong self-confidence, even though he has come out the obvious winner in the battles of deceit with the equally crafty Laban. He has become rich, owns many animals, and has a large family of eleven sons. He starts to go back to the land promised as his inheritance. The nearer he gets to Canaan, the more he breaks down. Fear sneaks back into his life when he realizes that he will have to meet Esau, whom he has robbed. Despite being his twin, Esau had vowed to kill Jacob for his treachery.

Jacob sends word to his brother that he's returning, and his servants carry lavish gifts of appeasement. As Jacob draws closer, he's still scheming and has already put emergency plans into effect. He divides his family into two groups. He takes extreme measures and willingly sends much of his wealth and property ahead to Esau to propose reconciliation. This no longer looks like the fearless Jacob we saw before. Neither is this a man who knows God or who is secure in his faith. Genesis 32 portrays him as a man plagued by doubt and terror. His gloom doesn't disappear when he passes Bethel, though he certainly remembers the promises given there by God.

For the first time in his life, Jacob seems deeply uncertain of his ability to deceive and win over an opponent. He has become the underdog, and fear guides his decisions. No matter what he offers, he has no assurance that bribes will bring peace with his brother. Jacob can't take God's blessings and help for granted. He feels as if he's on his own.

His desperate prayer, recorded in Genesis 32:9–12, indicates that something has happened. This time he doesn't bargain with God. We see none of the arrogance or self-justification that characterized him when he spoke to his wives, Rachel and Leah, or to Laban, in chapter 31.

The Holy has come to embrace him. Now Jacob has to face himself, or at least begin to. He confesses his unworthiness: "I am not worthy of the least of all the steadfast love and all the faithfulness that you have shown to your servant" (32:10). At last divine grace has broken through. Now he pleads for God's protection, afraid that his brother will kill them all, including the children. If that happens, the promises God had given Jacob years earlier won't be fulfilled.

At last the strange rewards begin to make sense.

At last Jacob faces his own image.

At last grace tackles Jacob and won't let go. Not that divine grace has ever let go; rather, Jacob has finally started to perceive God's undeserved presence. But it's not over yet. Confronted by God's majesty and power, Jacob responds this time in genuine repentance.

Then we read of an amazing occurrence, recorded in Genesis 32:22–32, where Jacob wrestles with the angel of the Lord. It goes like this: After sending his family and possessions ahead in groups, Jacob remains at a place he later names Peniel (32:30, "face of God"). He's greatly afraid and deeply troubled. No one else has remained, and he is totally alone. In darkness, he waits for daylight, and I imagine his mind could only conceive of the worst possible outcome.

He's ready to cross the river Jabbok, and then, still in the dark of night, Jacob encounters a powerful force. We have the impression that a man refuses to let him cross, so Jacob engages in an awesome struggle with his adversary, with the one he assumes is human. They wrestle, the man intent on preventing Jacob from crossing. The hand-to-hand combat continues until dawn, and neither gains mastery. At that point, the adversary throws Jacob's hip out of joint, but by then Jacob has guessed his opponent's true identity.

When the man asks to be released (perhaps because it's getting light and Jacob will be able to see him), Jacob says, "I will not let you go, unless you bless me" (32:26). The adversary blesses Jacob, and he is released. Later, when Jacob learns the name of the place, he is overwhelmed to realize that he had "seen" God face-to-face and survived. However, he doesn't escape untouched: For the rest of his life Jacob limped, a constant reminder of God's benevolence. Instead of killing him, God slowed him down with pain.

This is an amazing story, for it tells us that God appears to Jacob in human form, which is called a *theophany*. Several of these occur in the Old Testament, such as the appearance of the three men to Abraham in Genesis 18, or the military man who stands up to Joshua outside the walls of Jericho (Joshua 5:14).

No matter how we try to explain or understand this account, parts of it just don't make much sense. It's one of the instances where we do better not to push for a full explanation, but to ask a simple question: What's the point?

If we pull back a little and reconsider Jacob's original fearful night at Bethel when he fled from his brother's wrath, and then contemplate the next two decades, this struggle becomes the end of the tale. What happened during the intervening years? We have no record of God's being directly involved with Jacob. And yet God promised the blessings of children, wealth, and land. Eleven of Jacob's twelve sons were born while he was outside the Promised Land. God preserved his life, and now instead of being a fugitive with no possessions, Jacob returned as a man of vast wealth and a large family. Even more important, he returned to the land God promised him.

All of this makes me suspect that the quiet nudgings of God had been going on during those years, but Jacob hadn't listened. Surely Jacob has some twinge of guilt over his cheating, scheming ways.

I know this much: just before he crosses the Jabbok to go back into Canaan, Jacob finally has to examine his life. He has to confront himself, and that's where God comes in. He faces the Lord, and in that encounter he grasps a sense of his despicable nature. That divine-human encounter forces Jacob to stare at his own face. Something happened: God broke into his life and changed him.

Here's how I like to think of that struggle at the river: Jacob's fears, graphically stated in the first part of the chapter, so overwhelmed him that as he crossed the ford, he must have felt forsaken. God had rejected him—which he deserved.

Then comes the fight in the dark hours. In a moment of rare insight, Jacob realizes the identity of his adversary. It's not his twin, Esau—the one he has focused on as his enemy. He's been fighting God the entire time. God is the One who tries to stop him from crossing back into Canaan. Strange, in a sense, but the God who had promised Jacob the land is now the One who holds him back and refuses to allow him to enter.

Jacob's immediate reaction must have been to give up; he recognized himself as a conniving, shattered failure. Only a few hours earlier he had been brought to confess his worthlessness and see himself as he truly was, and perhaps even to hate himself for his sinful life. It's as if he will now get what he truly deserves. Yet there's something else: the fierce, bold Jacob awakens, and his fighting spirit asserts itself, as if to say, "I'm not going to let you get away with this."

He fights for his inheritance. One scholar calls it Jacob's "suicidal courage": "Bless me or I won't let go! I won't give up until you give me all the things you promised!" Although not the exact words, this attitude is what finally makes Jacob a true patriarch; he battles unrelentingly for the blessings of God. He wants—no, it's stronger—he must have what God had promised. He must receive the blessings that his own father Isaac had pronounced in God's name, and which he himself had so disgracefully won. Through all those wasted years in Mesopotamia, he had taken them for granted.

The "man" who wrestled all night with Jacob and refused to quit surely shows the relentless grace of God at work—the God who won't give up, the One who chases as long as it takes. Whatever happened, the story makes it clear that the patriarch limped away, a changed man.

Jacob may have seen this as his victory—and it was in the sense that he was changed. But it was really the victory of

God. At last the strange promise of reward makes sense: "So Jacob called the place Peniel, saying, 'For I have seen God face to face, and yet my life is preserved'" (Genesis 32:30).

This still isn't everything. We discern no radical shift in Jacob's behavior. We may secretly admire his cunning and persistence, but there's nothing in the man's life to genuinely embrace. This isn't the epic of a bad man who is transformed into a good man, as in the case of the Pharisee Saul who became the apostle Paul. It does, however, provide us with a story of a man of ferocious faith—one who, when forces assail, stands firm and refuses to surrender. This is the stirring action of faith within a man who, in many ways, behaves dishonorably; yet when we push away everything else and read how he faces God, Jacob stands tall as a genuine man of faith. His deeds aren't exemplary, and the Bible never portrays him as a sterling role model. It does, though, depict a man chosen by God—and the reasons for this may not make sense to us.

How can we ever understand why God would take a scoundrel like Jacob and bless him, make him wealthy, and let him become one of the great patriarchs of Israel? How could the Holy pursue a man most unholy? And not just pursue, but to chase him through two decades, never stopping, never relenting, always reaching for a man I would have given up on early in his life.

My way of responding is to look at my own life and see a

connection of the pursuing grace I have experienced, and I suspect that many of us could tell our own stories of how we ignored, denied, or ran from God. Then God caught us, and instead of hurtling our souls into damnation, He embraced us tightly and whispered, "At last."

The divine chase in my life sounds mild compared to that of Jacob, but the principle remains the same. As I mentioned earlier in this book, when I was ten or eleven years old, I went to Sunday school regularly for almost a year. Then I began to find it increasingly boring. I kept hearing the same stories and the same negative teaching about all the sinful things we were doing. I'd leave Sunday school convinced that I was racing toward the burning fires of hell.

My teacher, Marie Garbie, warned us almost every week about all the wicked things in the world. Everything I enjoyed doing, she taught against. I became convinced that I was going to go to hell anyway, so why not have a little fun along the way?

You will remember that during the time while I was still deciding whether I wanted to leave, Mrs. Garbie pulled me aside after Sunday school one morning. Her dark eyes bored into mine as she said, "God has his hand on you! God has a purpose for you, and you can't get away from it. You're going to serve the Lord in a wonderful way. And I'm already claiming part of the reward because I've been your teacher." She preached perhaps another five minutes, because she always seemed to say everything several times.

Then she grabbed my arm and took me to Brother

Newborn, our pastor. I could tell it was a setup, and that he had been waiting. They said they were going to pray for me to resist the evils of sin and serve the Lord.

I felt embarrassed to be at the front of the small church where people were starting to come in. They made me kneel down while they laid their hands on my head. It felt like they were holding me down so that I couldn't have moved if I tried. Soon others joined them. There must have been eight or nine people gathered around me, all of them praying aloud for God to keep me pure and good and to set me apart for divine service.

I hated that moment. I decided that once they let me go, I would never again return to that church.

Finally they stopped. All of them shook my hand or hugged me, assuring me that God would never let me get away.

I smiled and thanked all of them, but my smile and thanks were not genuine.

"Just remember," Mrs. Garbie said as I started to leave, "God's hand is on you, and he'll never let you go."

I didn't want the church, and I certainly didn't want God's interference in my life. I would surely become as boring or as crazy as the people who went to that church! That day was the last time I attended for at least a decade.

Eventually I felt a need for God in my life and did have a conversion experience. Once I believed, I went to visit Mrs. Garbie, then eighty-four years old. I told her I had turned to Jesus Christ.

"I told you God's hand was on you!" she said. "Do you remember that I told you God wouldn't let you go?"

Yes, I remembered. The first time she told me, her words had angered me. This time I rejoiced over the fact.

It's not that I mean to compare my life or my deeds to Jacob, but the divine purpose sounds remarkably the same. The Holy disrupts our lives for a reason. I believe that we can never successfully thwart God's purpose. Jacob ran for twenty years; I fled from God for ten. Eventually God caught up with both of us.

By contrast, my younger brother Mel ran for most of his life. God didn't catch up with him until months before his death from alcoholism, but then the Holy disrupted his life. Tanza Hobbs, a member of my Sunday school class, told us that she had run for years, and then one day, she said, "I met God and he stopped me cold. I knew it was my last chance to get my life straightened out and under divine authority." Many believers understand that part of Jacob's story, because it's much like their own.

Isn't that the way the Holy Pursuer often works in our lives? It's not based on our worthiness or our goodness. Sometimes I wonder if it's not because we are utterly unworthy, and finally admit this about ourselves. Once we perceive that we deserve nothing good from God, the Relentless Pursuer whispers, "At last." That's when we perceive who we've been, and we don't like it. We're ready to be divinely embraced.

Yes, and sometimes the rewards for the wicked seem strange. Or maybe that's just another example of God's extending grace to us, the undeserving.

CHAPTER FIVE

SEEING WHAT WE DON'T WANT TO SEE

W hy, God?

"Why are you doing this to me? What have I done to deserve such treatment?

"I've served you and followed you, and you bring all these things on me. Why, God, why?"

These cries sound remarkably common today. Yet they're also age-old laments from the earliest days of humanity. In fact, although not explicitly stated, they're the wails of a confused man named Job. We don't know when he lived. Some think as early as the first patriarchs of Israel, such as the time of Isaac or Jacob. Others place him in a later period, perhaps after the Jews' return from Babylon. Regardless of when the book of Job was written, it's a story all humanity can learn from.

The book begins by introducing a man "blameless and upright, one who feared God and turned away from evil"

(1:1). The story shifts to heaven where the Lord talks to Satan about Job and proudly reiterates, "There is no one like him on the earth, a blameless and upright man who fears God and turns away from evil" (1:8).

Satan insists that Job serves God only because of the blessings he receives: "Have you not put a fence around him and his house and all that he has, on every side?" (1:10). Satan challenges God to remove all protection and allow Job to be tested, alleging, "He will curse you to your face" (1:11). What Job didn't know—although readers do—is that God gave Satan power to test Job, and we're shown God's confidence that the righteous man won't surrender or yield to despair.

Although few people today get through all forty-two chapters (and they're not easy reading), most people know the basic story of Job's sufferings and about his ability to hold on when he loses everything, including his children, his health, his lands, animals, and wealth. As Job struggles with intense physical pain, his wife urges him to curse God, to give up and die. His friends come to comfort him and end up making him miserable and defensive. Other than death, there just isn't anything more that could have happened to Job.

That's the point, really. No matter how difficult anyone's life is, Job's life was more so. Job suffered more than most people suffer in an entire lifetime. Because of this, many have found solace in the midst of their own trials and losses. Job is a man to admire: he held on and maintained his innocence despite all the pointing fingers insisting he was a hypocrite and a terrible sinner whose wicked deeds had finally surfaced.

Job lived in a time when the idea was prominent that blessings and prosperity follow the faithful, while losses and troubles plague the wicked.

Once Satan got the opportunity to test Job, the man lost everything but his life. From there on, we hear no more of Satan. The back-story has lost its significance. Now we're struggling with a man who is righteous, and only slowly, as the story evolves, do we grasp something else: Job is also smugly self-righteous.

Job doesn't know this—yet. He can't know it until the Pursuing God catches up with him and enables him to see himself and to realize how small his view of the Holy really is. He's a man who does all the correct things, faithfully obeys in everything God requires, and lives a blameless life, but the inner Job hasn't been fully touched.

One of the significant messages in this book is about sin, even though it's not stated as strongly or clearly as it is in Paul's New Testament writings. All the participants in the book, including Job himself, are sinful. They're guilty of failing to follow God's holy path. Each of them, in his own way, paints a picture of God drawn from his own narrow, and consequently warped, understanding; each person insists on explaining God as if he has fully grasped all available knowledge. Each man seems unwilling to discover the true nature of the Holy and the divine purposes at work. In the end, God's self-revelation contradicts all of them.

Yes, there is sin, but something else in the story is even stronger. Above all, the true message of Job is grace. It's another picture of the relentless pursuit of the Holy to bring understanding to a few so that they may become role models for the rest.

For all of his abundant righteousness and his integrity, of which he himself speaks several times, Job is still a sinner, a kind of Adam in rebellion against the Creator. Basic to the book is that Job, who above all else wishes to be justified, learns that the way to justification isn't a do-it-yourself theology. He can't justify himself; he can only throw himself upon God's justifying grace. Justification isn't something to achieve; it's God's gift.

⟨❦⟩

Many words and events transpire before the Holy intervenes in Job's life, and it's easy to get sidetracked. Instead of emphasizing the man's suffering, I want to focus on his encounter with God.

The last chapter of the book finally allows us to see Job in a new light, an opportunity for him to stare at himself. This becomes a moment of self-revelation, and it's not pleasant. We read of a Job who's quite different from the man who defended himself against his well-intentioned friends. The one who had protested his righteousness now confesses, "Therefore I despise myself, and repent in dust and ashes" (42:6). These words come from a man who has finally gazed into the face of the Holy; he sees himself, and he is humbled. He no longer begs to be declared righteous.

The entire passage bears reading:

> Then Job answered the LORD: "I know that you can do all things, and that no purpose of yours can be thwarted. 'Who is this that hides counsel without knowledge?' Therefore I have uttered what I did not understand, things too wonderful for me, which I did not know. 'Hear, and I will speak; I will question you, and you declare to me.' I had heard of you by the hearing of the ear, but now my eye sees you; therefore I despise myself, and repent in dust and ashes" (42:1–6).

The book of Job teaches a subtle lesson. We know that Satan is behind all the ordeals that Job goes through: the death of his children, loss of everything he owned, and the rebuke and disgust of those he considered his friends. At the end of the story comes a shocking revelation that no matter what happens to us—and few of us have suffered like Job—God is in control. Job clearly recognizes divine sovereignty.

In chapters 38 through 41, God rebukes the patriarch, and the words reduce Job to silence. This isn't so much the surrender of a man who screams, "Okay, okay! I give up! Stop! Stop!" It is more of a willing capitulation. These are the words of a man whose eyes have been opened, and he sees what he hasn't wanted to see—himself.

Until this point, Job had focused on maintaining his innocence. No matter what his friends said or how loudly they protested that he was hiding the truth from himself, Job didn't listen. He knew he had done nothing wrong. He was sure of it. He focused on being mistreated and misunderstood, and he hinted at God's lack of concern.

Then comes the moment of self-revelation. He is arrogant, and the horror of that truth races through him. He had seen himself as a man condemned, and he sought justice from God. Finally, though, he realizes that his demands are worthless. By his surrender, Job entrusts himself to the Holy, whom he previously held responsible for his problems.

In 42:2, when Job confesses, "I know that you can do all things, and that no purpose of yours can be thwarted," he isn't making a trite theological point. He isn't cringingly confessing, "Oh, Lord, I'm nothing and only you can save me." He admits that only God can bring about justice. God opens his eyes to the massive presence of evil in the world.

Yet even in this display of divine power, we must not miss another significant factor: God opens Job's eyes to see his own wretched inner self. The protestor of innocence experiences a sense of his utter failure and contrasts that with God's great power. He doesn't understand God. In fact, if anything, he now *understands* less about God. Now he *knows* God, and this knowledge has been grasped through painful experiences.

Job has finally arrived at the place where he admits he has spoken of things he doesn't understand (42:3) and about things he can't control. With what little he does understand, he knows he has launched an indictment against God's character. In his humbled position, he accepts the reality that the divine nature as well as the disposition of rewards and retribution is ultimately beyond human comprehension.

There is an often-missed element to Job's confession: God cares less about our understanding of divine things than about our relationship with the Divine One. It is Job who matters, not his intellectual satisfaction or his theological grasp. The great conclusion is that Job ends the story having a deeper relationship with God. Intimacy is what matters ultimately.

"But now my eye sees you" (42:5) doesn't refer to a mystical experience. Job has faced God as a Being—no longer an object to discuss or argue about or a great truth to comprehend. He has experienced a personal encounter that wasn't evident before. Until now, it's as if God was some impersonal Creator, a force out there who cared, but whose caring was objective, detached, and impersonal.

How does this open-eyed experience affect Job? We find no statement such as "Peace swept through my heart" or "Unutterable joy filled my lips." Rather, this divine invasion left Job overwhelmed with a sense of his own incompleteness—his creatureliness. He saw himself facing Yahweh, the Almighty One. At that moment he confessed, "I despise myself, and repent in dust and ashes" (42:6).

His repentance wasn't for sins such as those with which his friends had charged him. There is no moment when he raced out to make restitution for his secret wrongdoing. It's not enough to say that he repented of his pride, which he surely did. He perceived himself as a creature, a human being, an object of divine love—and that God is Wholly Other.

Rather than vindication on his own terms as he desired, begged for, and confidently expected, he repents. Job stands somewhere between the Garden of Eden and the New Testament assurance of salvation by faith. He is a convicted sinner, not because of breaking specific laws, but simply because of his humanity.

As a sinner, he is embraced and loved by the same God who called to Adam, "Where are you?" (Genesis 3:9). That same voice calls to Job. The loving pursuit and ultimate embrace of God not only vindicates the man before his judgmental friends but it also humbles him. The point is that no one walks away unscathed from such an encounter with the Holy.

After seeing the shape of God in the clouds of the whirlwind and hearing heavenly words through the thunder, Job despises himself. Such a statement both uplifts and casts him down. He has seen the holiness of God, which he had known previously only through hearsay. Now that Job is confronted by the Holy, he weeps bitter, regretful tears, because he had made so much of his own righteousness and so little of God's holiness. He had harbored the thought that God is more interested in might than right, with little concern for justice.

What his friends have done in horror by tearing their robes and throwing dust on their heads (2:12), what Job himself has complained of God unjustly doing to him by casting him into the mire and making him like dust and ashes (30:19), Job finally does to himself in willing contrition. His pride has been deflated. He bows in humility as a creature before the Creator. Job is no longer obsessed with his own goodness or upright character.

Job's virtue has been acknowledged, and he hasn't been forced to confess sins he didn't commit, as his friends insisted he would. He also learns that none of us dares to presume on our own goodness. Suffering comes to the best of God's people, even if we can't explain the reasons behind the hardships.

God hadn't been arbitrarily and maliciously persecuting him, and Job (42:8) does intercede for the three friends who caused him so much pain. He no longer needs to scream out about his integrity. His depression has vanished, and the great burden of sadness and resentment has fled. Not all his problems have been solved, but he is able to view them in a larger and more hopeful perspective. A man who yearns to know everything has learned to live with ambiguity and uncertainty.

Job, in typical Old Testament fashion, viewed God as totally sovereign, and in his mind this made God, the Creator, responsible for all tragedies. But "then the LORD answered Job out of the whirlwind" (38:1), which turns the man's mind from brooding on how evil enters the world and moves it to the more practical question of how God gets rid of that evil. Job believes that, regardless of the power and threat of the enemy, nothing hinders God's eternal purposes. The man's words come as a cry of faith, and they come from having experienced deep distress before God opened his eyes.

Isn't this one of the less-than-subtle ways the Holy encounters us through relentless pursuit? We're the good people in our neighborhood, the ethical people at work, the nice people in social situations. We talk about Jesus Christ our Savior and live a fairly consistent life. The problem is that we often separate our inner selves from our outer behavior. We put our efforts on outwardly being good and ignore our inner needs. We live the external life of the believer, but do we feed our internal life?

I'll illustrate what I mean. I have a close friend named Mike, and he is highly respected in his field of work, at his church, and among those who know him. Yet Mike confessed to me, "The only time I pray is during the eight-minute drive from my house to my office. I run on spiritual near-empty all the time." He also said, "I can't remember the last time I sat down and actually read from the Bible."

My purpose isn't to push a form of behavior, such as a self-improvement program of praying, Bible reading, and church attendance, because that takes us back to outward conformity. My point is that Mike, like Job of old, has been looked upon as a spiritual or godly man. Only recently, when the Holy Pursuer caught up with Mike and forced him to examine his life, did he see the shallowness there. "I got so busy being good that I neglected being godly," he lamented.

Maybe many of us need to be grabbed and held by Holy hands and forced to look at ourselves so that we, too, may make the same statement.

CHAPTER SIX

LIVING WITH OURSELVES

An Atlanta newspaper carried the story of a thirty-three-year-old female driver who ran over a five-year-old boy. It was one of those accidents that couldn't have been prevented. She was cruising below the thirty-mile-an-hour speed limit down a tree- and shrub-lined street. Just before she reached her turn, the child darted out in front of her. Instinctively, she slammed on the brake pedal and spun the wheel away from him. It was too late. The side of the car caught the child and knocked him against the pavement. By the time she got out of the car and reached him, the boy had died.

The investigating officers didn't charge her, and the grieving family held no grudges against her. However, two months after the accident, she took her own life. Her suicide note read: "I can't live with this any longer."

As I've thought about this woman, it's made me consider

the consciences of those who by accident either kill or inflict serious physical injury. They have to live with what they have done. Every day of every year, they have to face their actions. How do they do that? Therapy can help. A solid relationship with the loving and forgiving God does even better. What about those who are haunted by their misdeeds?

I read a news item about a woman named Kathleen Soliah, a former member of the Symbionese Liberation Army. Apparently, in 1975, she placed pipe bombs under two Los Angeles Police Department squad cars. Although they didn't go off, Ms. Soliah fled, moved to Minnesota, married, had children, and lived like a normal, middle-class American for nearly thirty years under the name of Sara Jane Olson. In one TV interview, she said that she had tried to forget about her past, but that no matter how much she tried to push away the memories, they were always there. Like others who have escaped punishment for crime, she could not escape herself.

Then I thought about Moses. As a young man and an adopted member of Pharaoh's royal household, he murdered an Egyptian. This story gets little attention when people talk or teach about the great lawgiver; they usually mention it almost casually as a way to explain why he ended up in the country of Midian. Even the writer of Exodus states only that he killed the man and fled. When Moses returned years later to face Pharaoh (even though it was a different pharaoh), the subject doesn't come up. I've often wondered why.

The story, recorded in Exodus 2:11–25, tells us that Moses, who was born a Hebrew, was raised in the palace of

Egypt's ruler. His mother acted as his wet nurse, so we assume she told him of his heritage and kept alive the plight of his people, who had become the slaves of the Egyptians. After Moses had grown into manhood, "he saw an Egyptian beating a Hebrew, one of his kinsfolk. He looked this way and that, and seeing no one he killed the Egyptian and hid him in the sand" (2:12).

The story goes on to say that the next day Moses observes two Hebrew men fighting. To the one who was wrong, he asks, "Why do you strike your fellow Hebrew?" (2:13).

"Who made you a ruler and judge over us?" the angry worker responded. "Do you mean to kill me as you killed the Egyptian?" (2:14).

Fear gripped Moses, and he ran away to Midian. The Bible says that Pharaoh heard, and "he sought to kill Moses" (2:15). Then we have a brief paragraph about Moses becoming a shepherd, getting married, and fathering children. The king who sought Moses' life died, and chapter 2 of Exodus concludes by saying that the Lord "looked upon the Israelites, and took notice of them" (2:25).

From there the story zooms into the incident of the burning bush and God's calling Moses. But what was going on with Moses all those years? Did he—could he—forget so easily? Did his rationalization that he had killed an enemy of his people enable him to banish it from his memory? Did he ever think about what he had done? He had taken a human life!

Many skip over this part and say that life wasn't quite as meaningful to people in those days. I don't agree. Human life has always been precious, and murder has always been murder. Had it happened in war, it would have been different. Moses, however, deliberately killed an Egyptian because the man, probably under Pharaoh's orders, mistreated an Israelite. Could Moses have been so callous that the incident meant nothing to him? Was fear of punishment the only thing that troubled the future leader of Israel? If the story stopped there, this would be the most obvious assumption.

However, as we read more of the life of Moses in the books from Exodus through Deuteronomy, we find a picture of a different kind of person. Where is that hotheadedness and that quick temper that rages easily? In his zealous anger for God and his fury over the sinful behavior of the people, Moses threw down and broke the tablets containing the Ten Commandments. Another incident speaks of his temper, when after repeated complaints and agitation from an ungrateful mass of humanity, he strikes a rock with his staff to get water for them to drink.

The other stories of Moses, however, show him as calm, obedient, teachable. At one point, God refers to him as the most humble man on the face of the earth (Numbers 12:3).

Once we have seen the future Moses in action as God's leader, the burning bush story becomes even more significant. Not only is it about God's call for Moses to serve, it has to be more. Doesn't it make sense to believe that there has to be a story of Moses being forgiven? A point where Moses hears the voice of God say, "Your sins will not be held against you"?

Surely God isn't ignorant of the murder, and divine justice couldn't ignore it.

What happened? What turned Moses into a patient leader? How did the hotheaded zealot become the wise, impartial man who followed God in leading a rebellious nation over a period of forty years?

We don't know what or how, but we do know that something changed Moses.

For me, the story of the burning bush suggests far more than God calling Moses into leadership. Within this story, I see a holy encounter that's so powerful and so life-changing that Moses couldn't possibly have put it all into words. I suspect that the Holy Pursuer chased the man every day of his life. Like Kathleen Soliah, a.k.a. Sara Jane Olson, surely he thought of his evil deed every day of his life. In fact, in those moments when God encounters human beings, words become inadequate to explain an inner process. When God appears to his chosen one through a shrub that refuses to be consumed, the account is too powerful and too overwhelming to dismiss it only as a divine call. And it's possible that the fugitive had been running away from smaller, less intense burning bushes for forty years.

The third chapter of Exodus has a lovely simplicity about it; it is a story that puts us into the commonplace of Moses' life. He is doing what he had been doing every day: protecting his sheep. Assuming that area of Midian is a place of intense heat and that the incident takes place in the middle of the day, for a man to see the spontaneous ignition of a dry thornbush wouldn't have been altogether unusual. What makes it unique is that the flame continued to burn without consuming the bush.

Moses spotted the burning shrub, and no doubt wondered that it wasn't destroyed, or that the fire didn't go out. Under ordinary circumstances, a fire that continued would have ignited nearby bushes as well. Moses moved closer to gaze at the sight, and that's when God caught up with him.

Such an incident reminds us that the invasion of the Holy Pursuer often comes in these moments—an interrupting of our normal routines, when we're not prepared for a divine encounter. Most don't have the unusual setting this story does, but they can be every bit as dramatic.

In this account, Moses hears his name called as he moves closer to the bush. God speaks, and Moses recognizes who it is. "Come no closer!" the voice says. "Remove the sandals from your feet, for the place on which you are standing is holy ground" (3:5). In the East, removing their sandals was a sign of respect. This is probably why slaves went barefoot. God doesn't command Moses to remove his head covering, because that would have been a mark of equality.

In Exodus 3, we learn the message God speaks to Moses. Essentially it's a powerful moment of divine self-revelation and the commission of Moses. But that isn't all.

Moses' immediate response was "Here I am." When God spoke further, "Moses hid his face, for he was afraid to look at God" (3:6). Of course, there is the sense of awe at being in the presence of the Lord, even though Moses saw nothing other than the unconsumed bush. He perceived that God was present and communicating with him.

I hesitate to read into Scripture words that are not contained there, so I can only conjecture that somewhere in the midst of that experience the relationship changes between Moses and God. If Moses is the sensitive man we read of elsewhere, he must have intuited or even heard a message of "Your sins are forgiven." This must have been a time of reconciliation before the moment of divine commission, because throughout the Old Testament, God cleanses before commissioning. Especially when we consider the enormity of the task—to go before Pharaoh and eventually lead the people out of slavery into the land that God has promised—something must have taken place. Surely the Holy erases every barrier.

If this had happened to me, I think I would have been so overwhelmed with guilt and fear because of my wrongdoing, especially for having murdered the Egyptian, that I'd have needed some heavy reassurance that God had removed my sinful past before I could hear anything else. Consequently, I believe this abbreviated account implies a powerful moment when the Divine Chaser grabbed the man who had run for forty years, stopping him at last.

This is the face-to-face with God, the moment Moses sees himself as he is. Later Moses has other intimate experiences with Yahweh. God speaks directly to him in the wilderness and does it differently with Moses than with Aaron, Miriam, or anyone else. Moses holds a special relationship as a divinely chosen servant; because of this, it is obvious that the Holy has encountered and changed him.

After the divine command to go before Pharaoh, Moses doubts. At least he raises objections. My sense is that even if he had gotten the message of forgiveness, it was too quick and too much for him to absorb. If he lived for forty years in his shepherding occupation, constantly plagued with guilt and shame, surely the effects would not have vanished instantly. In the process of taking in both divine forgiveness and a divine commission, Moses raises at least four objections to his becoming the deliverer:

- "Who am I that I should go to Pharaoh, and bring the Israelites out of Egypt?" (3:11).
- "If I come to the Israelites and say to them, 'The God of your ancestors has sent me to you,' and they ask me, 'What is his name?' what shall I say to them?" (3:13).
- "But suppose they do not believe me or listen to me, but say, 'The LORD did not appear to you'?" (4:1).
- "O my Lord, I have never been eloquent, neither in the past nor even now that you have spoken to your servant; but I am slow of speech and slow of tongue" (4:10).

God dismisses each excuse.

Let's think about those disclaimers. If the Relentless Pursuer had not stopped Moses and dealt with him in such a way that cleansed and changed him, could these have been the only objections? Surely there would have been at least a fifth one, and it would have tumbled from his lips first: "I can't go. I'm a murderer and unfit to stand before the people. They know. They'll accuse me, or at least remind me."

We have no record of that excuse. Instead, Moses asks what makes him worthy to appear before Pharaoh. We read of no blurting out of his sin or his fear that this present pharaoh knows of his murderous deed. That seems totally out of Moses' mind.

If the Holy had touched Moses, the assurance of divine forgiveness would have been taken care of. That's why I think the story implies an even more powerful encounter—an experience of forgiveness. The objections then become those of inadequacy, not sinfulness.

If God caught him at the burning bush, let's consider the implications. He received forgiveness, of course, because Moses' sin has been wiped away. In addition, God not only cleans the blotted character but also calls the shepherd to an outstanding ministry. As we read of the words between God and the man, we also realize that this is a servant who soon overcomes his fear of talking to God and of doing the divine will. True, much of it involves offering excuses, but even that implies a relationship. It's a relationship and even a form of commitment by the newly called servant. It tells us that Moses believes God, but that he tries to explain why he can't perform the tasks.

The book of Hebrews makes this insightful statement: "By faith [Moses] left Egypt, unafraid of the king's anger; for he persevered as though he saw him who is invisible" (11:27). What a momentous change in this murdering, frightened man! He has been altered because the Holy has broken into his daily routine, held him tightly, and said, "I want you." Moses must have been offered forgiveness and accepted it.

This passage is about God calling Moses, and the events of Exodus depend on the clarity of this account. Within that call, however, I assume that the Holy touches Moses, assures him of divine forgiveness, and then prepares him for service.

This becomes significant in view of the divine self-revelation. In the Hebrew text, God uses the word *Yahweh* (or, as the older versions translate it, *Jehovah*). It's a word we can't pronounce because the Hebrew Bible contains only consonants; in this text, there are four of them: YHWH. Because of the expense of writing on skins, the scribes wrote the earliest manuscripts in block letters with no spaces between words and no vowels. To complicate this, from the time of their return from Babylon, pious Jews refused to speak that sacred name and substituted *Adonai* ("Lord"). In almost every English translation, though, we can see when YHWH appears because translators always render it in small caps: LORD.

What does YHWH mean? In Exodus 3:14, the word appears, and scholars have difficulty finding a way to explain it. Sometimes they have God saying, "I AM WHO I AM," which they usually put in small capital letters. Sometimes they translate it as "I WILL BE WHAT I WILL BE" or "I CAUSE TO BE." By using YHWH in personal reference, we assume God is saying something like this: "I am the Eternal One who is, was, and ever shall be." Nevertheless, instead of being caught up in the proper translation, it's more important to grasp that it's a special name: YHWH refers to the covenant-making God—a unique name reserved only for those who are part of God's unique people.

Yahweh tells Moses it's time to relieve the sufferings of the Hebrews, so it's a way of saying to him, "I have touched you, and now you are ready to go into the world and touch others."

This commission reminds me of the words of Paul when he writes to the Corinthians, "He comforts us when we are in trouble, so that we can share that same comfort with others in trouble. We share in the terrible sufferings of Christ, but also in the wonderful comfort he gives" (2 Corinthians 1:4–5 CEV). It's a message of comfort, and yet I believe this story suggests even more.

This incident implies not only that we have been comforted and can use that experience with God to console and encourage, but it also carries the idea of empathy. From this story, I think the Holy so captures Moses that he's never the same again. Not only does God change him—we expect that—but Moses changes in that he can offer others what he has received. Because the former fugitive has committed the most heinous of sins by societal standards—the taking of human life—and has now been embraced by the Holy One, how could he not now feel and understand the problems and hardships of others?

Moses being called the humblest man on the face of the earth later on shows that he grasped the enormity of facing the Holy. He sees not only himself and his deeds, something that he must have lived with every moment of his life, but he also moves beyond forgiveness. Yahweh, the Holy, has embraced him and commissions him to lead the people, entrusting him with the giving of the holy words, the Ten Commandments.

The point of this story of holy pursuit, and all such accounts, isn't so much the event but the effect: What happens after the experience? How are the individuals changed? Not only have they been confronted, but also they are able to accept the worst about themselves and offer acceptance and forgiveness to others. Encounters with the Holy lead not only to deeper commitment but also to showing the effect of the encounter through service.

I find it amazing that despite all the people that defy Moses afterward (including his own brother and sister), the constant rebellions, the renegade priests Nadab and Abihu (who offered "strange fire" to God), Moses remains the man of Yahweh. That flaring anger rarely shows up again. He not only understands others but he also accepts their fragility. He cries out to God on their behalf. Yes, Moses has been encountered by the Holy.

Today when we pray, "Forgive us our debts (or trespasses) as we forgive others," we're embodying the spirit of Moses. We're saying, "Holy One, you have rescued me and shown me myself, changed me, and in so doing, I have understood grace. Because I've understood grace, I can forgive those who sin against me."

CHAPTER SEVEN

MISSED BLESSINGS

"Would God really use an evil person to prophesy the future?" I asked that question when I was still a wide-eyed new believer. "Balaam is a pagan, and yet he prophesies future blessings on God's people. How can this be?"

"God chose to use him," the pastor answered in our Bible study. "We should never limit God's choices."

Although I heard his response many years ago, I still believe in the words of that pastor. At the same time, I have to admit that I don't fully understand the Balaam story, and I'm not sure anyone else does either. It's a long account that covers three chapters in the book of Numbers (22–24). It may help if I give a quick rundown of the events.

The Israelites have come out of Egypt, wander in the wilderness for years, and are now moving toward Canaan. "Moab was in great dread of the people, because they were so numerous; Moab was overcome with fear of the people of Israel" (22:3).

Balak, king of Moab, sends for a prophet named Balaam and commands him to curse the Israelites. Balak fears that they will fill the land; that is, they will become so numerous that they'll take over. The Jews are stronger, and Balak's army can't defeat them, but he believes that "whomever you bless is blessed, and whomever you curse is cursed" (22:6).

In those days people invoked curses against any who opposed them; we have a wide number of examples of this. We may choose, as many do, to see this as an expression of desire for God (or the gods) to share Moab's conviction to destroy the enemy. Regardless of how we think today, many ancients believed that curses and blessings, once pronounced, went into effect and could not be revoked. An example of this is that after Isaac blessed Jacob, the younger son, instead of Esau, and then learned that Jacob had tricked him, he could do nothing. Isaac said that the blessing, even if given to the deceiver, could not be undone.

Such was the understanding of that time period. Thus Balak believed that if he could get Balaam to curse Israel, the people of Moab would be safe from the approaching horde.

Confident of Balaam's ability to curse, a delegation goes to the prophet with "fees for divination" (22:7). This simply means they have come prepared to pay for him to curse their enemies. It was a well-established custom that prophets received payment for invoking blessings, cursings, or providing guidance from God (or the gods).

Here's where the story gets strange. Balaam says, "Stay here tonight, and I will bring back word to you, just as the LORD speaks to me" (22:8). *He uses the name Yahweh.* I find it strange that a man of Moab, someone not of the covenant family, would pray and talk to Israel's God and use this name, which was restricted to Israel. Then the story gets stranger. God answers Balaam's prayers and forbids the prophet to go with Balak: "You shall not curse the people, for they are blessed" (22:12).

Here are the possibilities. Some have suggested that Balaam was a secret worshiper of Yahweh, and therefore a friend of Israel. The Bible nowhere hints of this. Another theory says that Balaam consulted all the local gods and even consulted Yahweh, the God of the Israelites. That is, he asked every one of them. A third suggestion is that this is one of those occasions where Yahweh self-reveals to non-Israelites, such as to Jethro in Exodus 18, or to King Cyrus, who is referred to as God's anointed in Isaiah 45:1.

My theory is that the Sovereign God breaks into Balaam's world and speaks to him. As my former pastor said, "We should never limit God's choices." The seer receives a revelation from heaven and informs Balak that the divine plan can't be thwarted: God has chosen to bless Israel.

The passage goes on for a long time, and Balaam makes several shifts in his actions, but he never moves away from the basic fact that Yahweh has forbidden him to curse Israel. When Balaam answers King Balak negatively—and that must have been a fearful thing to do—he won't back down or be intimidated. This is truly an amazing stance of faith; the pagan prophet knows what Yahweh has declared and that it will come to pass.

Balak apparently assumes Balaam's refusal to go with him to curse his enemy reflects greed and that the Moabites aren't paying him enough. A delegation, therefore, makes a "great honor" (22:17), which is probably a matter of offering the man more money. Such an approach says Balak believes that if he makes the incentive big enough, Balaam will give in and do as he asks.

Balaam then makes a remarkable statement, a powerful testimony for God: "Although Balak were to give me his house full of silver and gold, I could not go beyond the command of the LORD my God, to do less or more" (22:18). The idiom "do less or more" is typically Hebrew and means simply that he can't do anything without having the Lord command him.

Even so, Balaam asks the delegation to spend the night while he prays again to Yahweh. This is confusing for Bible readers, because God has already told him not to go. God speaks again and the prophet is now commanded to go, but the Lord adds, "Do only what I tell you to do" (22:20).

The rest of chapter 22 is the famous story of Balaam and the ass. Three times, the donkey sees an angel and tries to get out of the way. In a rage, Balaam beats the animal, and then he too finally glimpses the angel, who stands before him with a drawn sword. The angel opposes Balaam because "your way is perverse before me" (22:32).

At those words, Balaam repents and offers to return home, but the angel tells him to go on and that he must speak, but only the words God gives him.

King Balak hurries to Balaam and chides him for not responding sooner, and then makes a little speech that emphasizes his own sense of self-importance. Balaam reminds the king that he can speak only what God has given him to say (22:38).

After that Balaam prophesies four oracles (chapters 23 and 24). Despite Balak's desires, Balaam absolutely cannot curse the people. The Israelites are the special nation of God, and he can't utter words of destruction against them. Balaam tries again and says that God isn't "a mortal, that he should change his mind" (23:19).

The third oracle begins with Balak in a panic, and he begs Balaam, saying in effect, "If you can't curse them, at least don't bless them." Balaam holds firm, refuses to add a curse, and speaks words of blessing. The incident ends with Balaam going back to his own home.

It's an odd story that offers little interpretation of the facts. Beyond this, we read Balaam's name three times in the New Testament, always negatively—the writers solidly condemn him.

"Why would they do that?" is another question I asked my pastor in those early days. "Balaam did what God told him to do, and then he's vilified in the New Testament for obeying. That doesn't make sense."

My pastor wasn't able to give me a satisfactory answer; I'm

not sure there is one. Here's my way of looking at this. The Holy pursues this man, speaks to him, and gives him the ability to see part of God's plan for Israel. A reading of the oracles provides an immense amount of insight about what Yahweh is doing and going to do with the people. Balaam receives the message and transmits it.

We have to commend Balaam for standing firm and obeying the command not to curse the people even when he must have feared the repercussions from King Balak. He faithfully speaks everything God says, but what does this do for Balaam? We find no evidence of a change of attitude or a confession that he is walking with God. We know nothing more about him from this portion of the Bible; we have to move into the New Testament to get the rest of his story.

Peter writes of false teachers who have gone astray after the way of Balaam (2 Peter 2:15). Jude refers to backsliders and says, "Woe to them! For they go the way of Cain, and abandon themselves to Balaam's error for the sake of gain" (Jude 11).

The curse of Balaam becomes clear in Revelation 2:14, which refers to members of the church in Pergamum who "hold to the teaching of Balaam, who taught Balak to put a stumbling block before the people of Israel so that they would eat food sacrificed to idols and practice fornication."

This last verse comes as a bit of a shock because there is no such Old Testament reference. It reinforces my question: What change occurs in Balaam after his encounter with the Holy?

Perhaps it helps if we think of the modern world and ourselves. Is it possible that the Holy can touch individuals in supernatural ways and yet the encounter makes absolutely no change in their behavior? Does the Pursuing One touch lives, and then they live as if they had never experienced the holy presence? Can we conceive of God making individuals spiritually alert—aware of their needs, conscious of the way of peace and righteousness—and they return to the old way of life?

The best illustration I know of this took place when I was a pastor, perhaps a year or so before anyone talked about what we now call near-death experiences. A woman I'll call Rebecca came to church perhaps four times a year; even she said it was for social reasons, as she had little interest in God or religious matters. Then Rebecca faced death with a serious heart ailment, which was discovered when she visited the doctor with a different complaint. She went in to surgery the next day, and I visited her hospital room before and afterward.

"I had a strange experience," Rebecca told me the day after the surgery. She reported a sense of leaving her body and floating above the operating team. She watched them work. One of the doctors had brought in his tape recorder and played Bach's "Brandenburg Concerto."

"We've lost her," a nurse said.

Frantic activity went on, and she felt herself drifting from the room and into a dark passageway. "I became aware of all the wrong things I had done, and I began to cry and beg God for another chance. I saw the face of Jesus staring at me. He told me that he had died for me and that he loved me. Once I asked God to forgive me, I saw a light—a tiny ray—far ahead." She saw herself racing across a meadow, rushing toward that light. "The closer I got to the light, the more peaceful I felt. I've never experienced such a calmness and contentment before." Seconds before she actually walked into the light, something jerked her backward, and she felt thrust into her body again.

That afternoon, the doctor came in and told her, "We almost lost you on the operating table." She replied by telling him what she had seen, including hearing the music and the conversation. She even remembered that one of the nurses chewed gum during the surgery and that a doctor had kidded her about it.

For the six days Rebecca remained in the hospital, she talked about that incident. I saw a radiance on her face different from anything I'd observed before. As soon as she was physically able, Rebecca started attending church. She came nine Sundays in a row, which was a record for her. But she didn't come the tenth week or any other Sunday after that.

I visited her, but she made it clear that she didn't want me to call again. "I'm not interested," she would say as soon as I began to talk about God. On the last occasion, I said something about her meeting God. She shrugged. "That was months ago," she said, ending our discussion.

For a long time afterward, I kept asking myself, *How could that woman have been so close to God and yet veer so far away?* I couldn't understand how a person could be so enlightened and not be changed forever. Obviously, it happens.

That's how I perceive the story of Balaam. He hears from God, in stronger, more powerful ways than many committed believers have ever experienced the divine presence. But what good does it do him? Balaam, and people like Rebecca, have been pursued, halted, and seen the face of the Holy. They experience God . . . and then what?

Having been educated in Reformed theology, I know all the orthodox answers that say those who have truly known God will persevere to the end—their perseverance is proof of their having believed. That may be so. I know only that there are some examples we can't explain.

I think also about one of the most gifted Africans I've ever met. His name was Joseph Otengo. When he preached, God spoke to people, and many surrendered their lives. On the occasions when we talked, his face and voice radiated the love and joy of Jesus Christ.

"I came to believe in your God," one woman told him, "because I can see Him in your eyes."

Yet later that same man indulged in several sexual affairs, an issue I had heard him preach against. In the end, he simply walked away from God and said he had lost interest. He died in an accident shortly afterward.

The evangelist had been touched by the relentless pursuit of the Holy. Joseph knew the way, walked in it, and pointed many others down the path of righteousness. In the end, however, he turned away. I can only assume that being enlightened isn't enough. Experiencing the gift of salvation (or whatever lesser terms others choose to use) didn't lock him into the grace of God.

I don't understand Balaam, and I don't understand Rebecca. I can't comprehend Joseph's attitude and behavior either. The stories of these three individuals sadden me. They remind me that when the Holy invades our lives and chases us through the events of our lives, the divine activity has a purpose. We're tapped by God and called to be transformed into being increasingly like Jesus Christ (see Romans 8:29). Although I find it abhorrent that people can close their eyes and shut out the Holy, and even though my theological background tells me that can't happen, my experience with others whispers, "Yes, it can."

What if there are those who are truly encountered by the Holy, and they turn away? They see themselves in the worst possible way and also grasp the loving, forgiving grace of God through Jesus. Then they avert their eyes and walk away. Is that possible?

Years ago someone said to me, "If you're not moving forward with God, you're not standing still, you're moving backward." Yes, I think going backward is possible, and only by the grace of God can we be held so tightly that we won't return. I simply don't have answers for such situations. But I find consolation in one fact: God pursues us.

I can't explain those who push aside grace or ignore the inexpressible compassion that attempts to embrace them. I can say that not only did God chase me but also that grace and love have pushed aside any desire to go back.

For at least the past decade I have paused each morning as I lie in bed, preparing to get up for the day, to give God thanks for at least ten things: "Thank you for loving me enough to pursue me even when I didn't want you," is one way I start my thanksgiving list.

CHAPTER EIGHT

PRESUMPTIVE GUIDANCE

Ken Bennett Jr. phoned me from the mountainous region of Pennsylvania where he had been a pastor for nearly a year. No matter what he did, attendance didn't improve; no strangers visited the church, and bulk mailings had no effect. "I believe God wants us to grow and to be a lighthouse to the community," were his words.

He called to tell me that he had rented a large tent and wanted me to come and preach for five nights, and asked that Shirley play the piano. I'm not an evangelist, but Ken assured me that if I preached, he'd give the call at the end, and the Holy Spirit would draw many unbelievers to follow Jesus Christ.

Shirley and I agreed to help him. The first night no one showed up except a dozen members of his congregation, but I preached anyway. The second night, no new people came. Two new people did attend the final night, but they were members of another church who came, they said, "to encourage."

Ken had taken in so little money from offerings that Shirley and I actually ended up paying for the rental of the tent instead of receiving an honorarium.

After the final service, Ken, very discouraged, wept and pleaded with God, unable to understand what had gone wrong. "I know this is right—to win souls for you. We gave ourselves to you and we visited and put up notices, but nothing happened." In his deep pain, on and on he went, always adding that God wanted to save souls, and how discouraged he was that no one had responded.

Who knows the reasons for lack of success in that venture? I could cite other instances of people trying their best for God and not seeing results. One comes to mind that I've never figured out.

When we served as missionaries in Kenya, we had an opportunity to start a church just over the border in Tanzania. We sent one of our most talented preachers, and several of us—missionaries and nationals—went to open-air meetings and church services to support him. Everything had pointed to that town as a prime spot. We had prayed and sought God's guidance. *Or did we seek God's guidance?*

We prayed fervently. I recall that several of us, excited for the opportunity, presumed that this was the proper move. The door had opened for us, and we hadn't asked for it. We had a fiery evangelist available. Everything seemed to fit, but the infant church failed. As far as I know, nothing ever came of our efforts.

Looking back, I wonder if we weren't guilty of presumptive guidance. That is, we were too positive we were doing the right thing at the proper time. Why wouldn't God bless our efforts? Why wouldn't we be able to accomplish great things through the intervention of the Holy Spirit?

I know only that presumptive guidance can be dangerously misleading. We assume we're doing the right thing. Are we? How do we know for certain?

I thought of the biblical account of Joshua and the people of Israel right after their victory at the great city of Jericho. Then, prepared for battle against the small town of Ai, they presume divine guidance and attack. The huge Israelite army runs away in defeat after thirty-six of their soldiers die. They had taken it for granted that God was leading them. After all, they had received the promise of an inherited land.

They merely presumed they had divine guidance; they didn't seek it.

After the routing, a discouraged Joshua prays, and God explains that there is "sin in the camp." Then the story comes out. A man named Achan has stolen and hidden gold, silver, and clothing after the battle of Jericho. God had forbidden them to keep any of the spoils, because they were to surrender everything as a sacred offering. Joshua doesn't know about Achan's sin until God reveals it; that is, until he prays and asks, "What happened?" The leader's problem is that he had presumed everything was all right when his soldiers moved into battle.

Presumptive guidance. When we assume we know what God

is doing or saying without hearing directly from the Source, we're in danger. Assuming to know God's will keeps doors locked tight against a divine entry or the invasion of the Holy. Obviously, the Holy Spirit can break into our lives and say, "Wait a minute." But why would we make it more difficult? Why wouldn't we ask first? Maybe it's easier to follow programs and patterns of guidance that have worked before than it is to be open to the soft nudging of the Holy Spirit speaking in the present.

I want to point to one more biblical story in the life of Joshua. This happens just before the battle for Jericho. Moses has died on the other side of the Jordan River; the people have ceremonially cleansed themselves, and they march across the Jordan and cross the border into the land. The walled city of Jericho is their first military objective.

The book of Joshua begins with several exhortations and promises from Yahweh to the new leader:

- "Proceed to cross the Jordan . . . into the land that I am giving [you]" (1:2).
- "Every place that the sole of your foot will tread upon I have given to you" (1:3).
- "As I was with Moses, so I will be with you; I will not fail you or forsake you" (1:5).
- "Be strong and courageous; for you shall put this people

in possession of the land that I swore to their ancestors to give them" (1:6).

- "Only be strong and very courageous, being careful to act in accordance with all the law that my servant Moses commanded you" (1:7).

- "Be strong and courageous; do not be frightened or dismayed, for the LORD your God is with you wherever you go" (1:9).

I've tried to figure out how I would have felt if I had heard all those wonderful assurances of victory. I'm sure I'd be anxious to get moving and displace my enemies.

Joshua follows God's leading and is a marvelous example of faithfulness: he makes all the preparations for moving forward, including circumcising all the males, setting up twelve memorial stones at Gilgal, and observing the Passover.

A brief interlude occurs before the people move toward Jericho. It's one of those stories that scholars have difficulty explaining. Most of the time they pass over the section, or they simply link it with the Jericho story of chapter 6. The translators of the NRSV call the story "Joshua's vision"; that is, they assume this didn't literally take place, but that when Joshua prayed he had a dream the night before the battle of Jericho.

I have no difficulty believing the incident literally happened, even if I don't fully understand it. Let's examine the story. Found in Joshua 5:13–15, the brief account tells us that Joshua is near Jericho, looks up, and standing before him is a man whose sword is drawn, ready for battle. The Israelite leader, staring at the battle-ready sword, asks the obvious question: "Are you one of us, or one of our adversaries?" (5:13). The man replies that he is the "commander of the army of the LORD" (5:14). Hearing this, Joshua falls to the ground and worships, and then asks, "What do you command your servant, my lord?" (5:14). The armed man tells him to take off his sandals, because he is in a holy place.

As I've pondered this story, I believe it is the Holy breaking into Joshua's life. It is a moment when the divine pursuit halts the leader to prevent presumptive guidance.

Consider all the assurances Joshua and the people have received. Before the death of Moses, God frequently points to the land of Canaan as a place of milk and honey—a fertile, desirable home. Yahweh has called them from Egypt and prepares them to enter into the land promised to Abraham and confirmed both to Isaac and to Jacob.

The first chapter of Joshua reads like a book of golden promises of God's presence, guidance, and power. What more does Joshua need to hear? The Israelites can't fail. Why won't Joshua charge forward, filled with faith and zeal?

God has promised the land, and now they're ready to march in and take it from their adversaries. Tucked within the promises is an exhortation:

> Only be strong and very courageous, being careful to
> act in accordance with all the law that my servant Moses
> commanded you; do not turn from it to the right hand or

to the left, so that you may be successful wherever you go. This book of the law shall not depart out of your mouth; you shall meditate on it day and night, so that you may be careful to act in accordance with all that is written in it. For then you shall make your way prosperous, and then you shall be successful. (1:7–8)

This directive may well be the purpose of the appearance of the man with the drawn sword. Here's where presumptive guidance comes in. Joshua, ready to rush forward and to do God's will, assumes that the soldier is either for or against Israel. He misses the point entirely. He faces a man, but the context makes it clear that this is one of those Old Testament theophanies—appearances of God in human form.

The man declares he isn't an ally or adversary, but "as commander of the army of the LORD I have now come" (5:14).

This is God breaking into Joshua's world. To the credit of the leader of Israel, he grasps this immediately. Again, here's how the Bible describes Joshua's response: "And Joshua fell on his face to the earth and worshiped, and he said to him, 'What do you command your servant, my lord?' "

That's the end of the story, but not the conclusion of the message. Compare this to the account of Moses: Both men worship, Joshua before the armed commander and Moses in front of the burning bush. Both are informed they stand on holy ground and must remove their sandals. They do exactly as they're told.

Although previously called and encouraged by God, Joshua's encounter with the commander is remarkably similar to Moses' experience. That fact alone may have been a message for the people as much as for Joshua himself. Even more significant, God speaks before the first battle. It's not enough for Joshua to know that God is with him or that the people will inherit the land. This story is the invasion of God into Joshua's life, an unexpected moment.

God is saying that Joshua must align himself with God; he can't presume that the Lord is pushing him to victory. It's not that Yahweh will withhold victory, but something more basic demands attention. It's the Holy saying, "Get in step with me. Don't ask me to give you victory and don't presume you'll succeed in this first battle or any of the others. If you follow me and do what I say, you'll receive all the good things I've promised."

Joshua grasps the message this time. The book of Joshua, unfortunately, also makes it clear that at least twice, on later occasions, he acts on presumptive guidance. I've already mentioned one: going into the battle of Ai. Before long Joshua and his people will attack the country of the Gibeonites.

The Bible says, "But when the inhabitants of Gibeon heard what Joshua had done to Jericho and to Ai, they on their part acted with cunning" (9:3–4). They go to Joshua and his leaders. To be convincing, they carry moldy bread and patched wineskins and wear their oldest clothes. Claiming they have come from a far country, they ask the Israelites to make a treaty with them. They hold out their spoiled bread as proof of their long journey and claim, "This was freshly baked just before we left." The Bible records, "So the leaders partook of their provisions, and did not ask direction from the LORD. And Joshua made peace with them, guaranteeing their lives by a treaty; and the leaders of the congregation swore an oath to them" (9:14–15).

No military battle takes place, but Joshua and the people open themselves to deception. The Hebrew leaders go forward on their own without allowing God to break in and guide.

Here's my assessment of Joshua and why I've included his story in this book. He was Moses' protégé. We learn of his military leadership at their first battle after leaving Egypt. Exodus 17:8–13 records the account of Joshua and the Israelite army defeating the Amalekites.

Certainly he was a brilliant military man, but other than this, I wonder what kind of man Joshua really was. If he had been a confident, self-assured leader, why would there have been so many verses of encouragement? Why would God have repeatedly needed to reassure him? (See again the promises in Joshua 1.)

Could it be that although he was an excellent military leader, he wasn't a man confident enough to lead the people of Israel into the land? Is it possible that Joshua might still be a man who raced forward on his own, not yet caught by the pursuing presence? Could he have needed an encounter with the Holy before he was ready to lead the people?

My assumption is that the description of the commander

with the drawn sword who stands in front of Joshua says something powerful. The sword shows a readiness and an ability to conquer. His message to Joshua is, "This isn't your battle because they are not your army. This is Yahweh's battle, and you will become victorious because I'm with you."

This moment when the Holy breaks through changes Joshua. As we read of his leadership from then on, we don't find those constant words, "Okay, Joshua, don't be afraid." Or "I'm with you just as I was with Moses."

"Take off your sandals," the commander says. That's the point of this story. After Moses faced the Holy, he changed. When Joshua faces the Holy, he changes. In both instances, the confronting voice calls the place "holy ground," but that isn't meant to be understood as a piece of sacred real estate. If it had been, both men would have erected memorials. Rather, it's God's way of saying, "You are in the presence of the Holy."

That's the significant moment: Joshua's realization that he's in a face-to-face encounter. The Pursuing Presence has caught up with him. Joshua struggles with presumptive guidance, as I've already mentioned. He obviously isn't of the same spiritual caliber as Moses, but he is the divinely chosen leader for the assault of the Promised Land. His meeting the commander, then, becomes the turning point. Except for the incidents of his presumptive guidance, Joshua serves God well and faithfully.

This isn't to belittle Joshua. Presumptive guidance plagues most of us. It's subtle, and it often runs contrary to common sense. Let's think about how it works.

"I know God, I read the Bible, and I live by Christian ethics," Al Antilla once said to me. "So why do I need to stop and pray over every tiny decision? I don't have to ask God if I need to go to work today. It's my job, so I go."

Obviously. Who would argue that? The problem arises when we begin to take guidance or divine grace for granted— when we think we always know what God wants. It's an assumption without knowing—another way of saying presumptive guidance.

Until the moment the man with the sword appears, Joshua thought of "us" and "them." Then he's forced to shift his focus to "God" and "others." God in human form encounters Joshua and pushes him to a point of realization that he isn't going forward by his own ability; only as the All-Wise One directs him can Joshua know that victory lies ahead. He seems to grasp the message, and the victory over Jericho follows.

Joshua slips after that, but not because of his personal sin. He fails because he doesn't seek God first. He assumes the next victory will be as outstanding as the previous one.

That's where we, like Joshua, get into trouble. We presume we know the way. When the Holy encounters Joshua, I believe the message is to enable the new leader to understand that *all* things are in God's hands. What the newly appointed leader doesn't seem to grasp is that it becomes an ongoing matter of hearing from God. He needs to hear before every battle, before every decision. Joshua, confident of victory the first time, presumes they will shout victory the second time.

When the Holy encounters us, it is to remind us of the words the sword-wielding soldier speaks: "As commander of the army of the Lord I have now come" (5:14).

As it was with Joshua, so it is with God's voice encountering us. Because we like to think that God is for us in everything we do, we forget that God's will comes first.

❧

The second incident of presumptive guidance begins with this statement: "So the leaders partook of their provisions, and did not ask direction from the Lord" (9:14). Three days after the leaders of Gibeon deceive the Israelite leaders, Joshua realizes their scheming, but he honors the treaty. The Gibeonites become "hewers of wood and drawers of water for the house of my God" (9:23). This is, however, the last time we read that Joshua makes the mistake of presumptive guidance.

Shouldn't this be a lesson to us that even when things seem obvious, we can't be sure until we've heard from heaven? The Holy encounters Joshua in a powerful manner, so strongly that he falls prostrate and worships. It still takes a couple of bitter experiences before the message impacts him.

That may be one of the best ways to remind us that we're not all that different from Joshua. The Holy may encounter, speak to us, make us aware, but the change doesn't always come instantly. Perhaps, like Joshua, we learn slowly.

As sad as Joshua's experiences are, I find a powerful message of hope. These almost-failures remind us that the Holy One never stops pursuing. The divine stalking persists to remind us that we're important to the Creator of heaven and earth, who "so loved the world that he gave his only Son" (John 3:16). And each of us is part of "the world."

CHAPTER NINE

MISUSED GIFTS

My younger brother, Mel, died more than a decade ago, and I still miss him. But aside from missing him, it saddens me to think about his wasted life. Of all the members of our family, his sharp mind and quick reflexes made him outstanding. He was two years younger than I, yet even during our growing-up years, I admired the giftedness of my brother.

For instance, a neighbor once threw away an alarm clock. Mel found it and took it apart, something he hadn't done before. He studied it, touched a few parts, bent several things, and put it back together. It ran perfectly for years. At the time he fixed the clock, Mel was about eight years old.

My brother had much to offer, and yet he didn't fulfill any of the promise that seemed so evident as a child. I've never understood why. It also puzzled me that he became the family rebel when he was still quite young. He died after years of alcohol abuse.

I mention my brother because one of the saddest things in life for me is to think of those who show so much promise but who don't live up to their abilities. Maybe that's also a reason why the entire book of Judges is a chronicle of grief for me: The repetitive cycle of sin, bondage, crying for help, the rise of a deliverer, a period of peace, and then the cycle begins again. One of the characters is Samson, and there is more about him in Judges than any other person (four chapters).

The extended introduction to Samson that begins in chapter 13 indicates that God expected much from this gifted leader. When an angel announces to his barren parents that they will have a son, it's not recorded as it is in other instances, such as to Hannah, Elizabeth, or Mary. Usually the story reads that the angel announces the event and gives the parents the child's name based on the role that person will play. This story is different. Instead of naming him, the angel emphasizes that the boy will become a lifelong Nazirite—a person who makes a sacred commitment or vow to God. Part of this forbids strong drink, eating anything unclean, and "no razor is to come on his head, for the boy shall be a nazirite to God from birth" (13:5).

Chapter 13 ends with an interesting note about Samson: "The boy grew, and the LORD blessed him. The spirit of the LORD began to stir him" (vv. 24–25).

Here we have a marvelous setup for a faithful man to serve God all his days. This has an even better beginning than the story of Samuel (see chapter 10), but the story doesn't end that way. This charismatic leader violates his vows. He chases women. He eats honey taken from the ritually unclean corpse of a lion.

The grand finale of Samson's life comes when he tells Delilah the secret of his incredible physical strength: It's because he's been a Nazirite since birth and no razor has ever touched his head. Later, while he's asleep, she calls in Philistines to shave him. When he awakens, the Bible says, "He did not know that the LORD had left him. So the Philistines seized him and gouged out his eyes. They brought him down to Gaza and bound him with bronze shackles; and he ground at the mill in the prison. But the hair of his head began to grow again after it had been shaved" (16:20–22).

The Philistines celebrate Samson's capture at a religious festival where they offer thanks to their god, Dagon, for delivering their great enemy. By the time of the feast, Samson's hair has grown.

The temple rests on pillars, between which the Philistines put the blinded hero. In that hostile place, away from his own people, is where the Holy Pursuer finally catches up with Samson. Until his betrayal by Delilah, this strong man has violated every one of his oaths and seems to be the kind who needs no one's help, not even God's. Yet it is at this place, in the presence of his enemies, that Samson finally stops running. At last the voice of the Holy speaks, and Samson responds. In his darkest moment, when he's blind and imprisoned, Samson utters the first formal prayer found in the four chapters of his story. There is a record of his crying out for water after he had killed a thousand Philistines (15:18), but this prayer is different. This is the wail of a humbled Samson. This is a man who's been caught, trapped at last by the Pursuing Lover of humanity.

It takes place only after he's been brought low, when he's absolutely helpless. He hadn't asked for the gift of immense strength, and the Nazirite vow had been laid on him before his birth. God's Spirit had always come when needed, apparently unasked. Finally, humbled and blinded, the butt of cruel sport, he acknowledges his need.

It's almost as if the Holy whispers, "Finally, Samson, you know yourself. And you know how much you need my help."

Samson prays, "Lord GOD, remember me and strengthen me only this once, O God, so that with this one act of revenge I may pay back the Philistines for my two eyes" (16:28). It's not the prayer we want to hear. We modern readers would like to see a lengthy section of confession of failure and recognition of his sins. This may have happened. In fact, I assume it did.

It's hard to imagine how else this scene could have taken place. Samson, divinely called to deliver Israel, failed repeatedly. He used his singular gift of physical prowess when needed in battle. However, he seemed never to have recognized his dependence on God. His is a life of running away from everything good and noble, and most of all refusing to align himself with the divine will. In the weeks, or perhaps months, while the blinded man ground at the mill, surely there was opportunity for the Holy to speak, to nudge, and to keep after him until he listened.

Samson's desire for revenge can distract readers, but he was a man whose physical strength filled his world. Killing the enemies of his people was his focus. As the Philistines' prisoner at Gaza, a humbled, blinded, and fettered Samson faced his vulnerability. His prayer was a far cry from that of Jesus or Stephen to forgive his oppressors. Even so, this may well have been a breakthrough for a person who had relied only on his own ability and talents.

I've met people like Samson. They become so caught up in their own strengths that they think they don't have needs like other people. They reek with self-sufficiency. During our missionary days in Africa, I worked with such a person whom I'll call Milt.

Milt wasn't well liked, but he was much admired. He knew more of God's plan for Africa than anyone (and if we had any doubts, he'd tell us). He was a man of great vision and seemed able to peer about ten paces ahead of everyone else. Milt was also ruthless and had little respect for others' needs. He showed great intolerance for failures or weaknesses.

One time I was in a meeting with him. Then just before we left, another missionary prayed that God would help Milt drive carefully. Milt mumbled, "I don't need to pray about that. All I have to do is slow down and watch the road." That may sound like a small thing, but it was typical of him because he seemed invulnerable.

On another occasion, Milt and I were in a meeting with five African leaders. I had been in the country only a few months and scarcely knew the language. Milt scolded me and made several disparaging remarks about my inability to speak Swahili. George Lindsay, the only other missionary present, walked across the room, sat down next to Milt, and said quietly. "You're wrong. You owe Cec an apology." Had I not been sitting near Milt, I probably wouldn't have overheard.

"Apology? For what?" Milt pushed the remarks aside and called me bumbling and ignorant, but the other man said, "No, you need to apologize. He did nothing wrong. You never explained things to him, and now you tear him apart. That's not right."

As far as I know, no one had ever confronted Milt. Everyone had always quietly taken his petty insults or smug remarks.

Milt's anger erupted, and words of self-justification poured out, but the confronter said nothing until Milt finished. "You still need to apologize."

Stronger, more vitriolic words filled the air. As I watched, George kept his eyes focused on Milt. Finally, he said softly, "You were wrong, and you make it worse by justifying your behavior."

Had George yelled in rebuttal, I think Milt would have shouted even more. Perhaps it was the quietness of his tone or the power behind his quiet conviction. Milt opened his mouth and then stopped. It was as if he had been struck dumb for several seconds. He stared at George and then turned to me. Moisture filled his eyes, but he said nothing.

I stared back, feeling uncomfortable and not sure what to say or do. Just then a tear slid down Milt's cheek. "I'm sorry," he said, and then he hugged me. "I've been wrong and . . ."

Great sobs erupted, and for several minutes Milt, who was at least half a foot taller and outweighed me by a hundred pounds, hugged me tightly.

I was shocked. The stories about the man's hardness were legendary. He didn't know it, but the Africans had a name for him that translated meant he was as hard as a hammer.

What happened in that meeting is beyond me to explain, except that the Pursuing Holy Presence touched Milt in such a way that it broke through his own defenses, his self-righteousness, and his formerly impenetrable shell. He changed toward me. Not that we ever became friends, but after that he treated me more kindly and with at least some respect.

Think about the man who was a hero to the people of Israel. Women flocked around him, and the people must have shrugged off his weaknesses because he was a man of unique talent and physical virility.

I know what happens when the Holy breaks through to the Samsons who haven't been listening. Even among Christians, I've observed those gifted individuals, truly charismatic and often brilliant. They seem endowed with unlimited ability. Why do they need to seek guidance? What do they lack? They have it all, at least for a while, but the original Samson lost it all. Yet in losing, he won. That's when the Holy captured him and he admitted his neediness: "Help me this one last time."

Our situations aren't usually this drastic, of course, but the principle holds true. Only when the Holy breaks through our resistance—only when we see that we aren't sufficient—can we then realize the strength of God in our lives. Only then do we perceive that the One we've run from is the One who truly cares.

God heard Samson's prayer. Here's what the Bible says: "Samson grasped the two middle pillars on which the house rested, and he leaned his weight against them, his right hand on the one and his left hand on the other. Then Samson said, 'Let me die with the Philistines.' He strained with all his might; and the house fell on the lords and all the people who were in it" (16:29–30).

Divine strength returns; Samson pushes, and the building collapses, killing him and everyone inside. A sad ending to his story, but it's also an ending that brings closure. The man has had supernatural strength all his life, and now, at the end, he finally faces the Holy; in so doing, I think he faces himself. What a miserable life he has led. He was a charismatic leader for twenty years, but what did those years count for? Judges says, "So those he killed at his death were more than those he had killed during his life" (v. 30).

Samson, like my brother Mel thousands of years later, wasted his gifts. And both of them faced the Holy only at the end of their lives. As I reflect on these two men, I wonder about something. What would Mel's life have been like had he stopped running when he was a teenager, or when he was thirty? How much more effective might Samson have been if he had not run from the Pursuing God?

CHAPTER TEN

CLAIMED BY THE HOLY

"I can't remember when I didn't love God," my wife, Shirley, has said many times. Her parents taught her from infancy to believe in Jesus Christ, and she did. Like other "cradle Christians," she's been a believer all her life and has no particular time she can mark as the moment when God began to work in her.

Others among us can point either to a crisis event, to a season, or to a definite moment of God's intervening in our lives. Few of us can go back to childhood and say something like, "When I was five years old, I trusted Jesus Christ as my Savior. Since that day, God has continued to speak to me and use my life to enrich others, and I have never strayed from the path." If we did talk this way, we'd probably sound vain or boastful.

There is one such person in the Bible, however. His name is Samuel, and his divine encounter is one of Scripture's best-known and most-loved stories. Samuel served God and never deviated. The voice of God speaking to the boy sets the stage for one of the great phases of biblical history.

A survey of the situation in Israel helps us grasp the power and intent of this story. The old man, Eli, is high priest, and the Bible refers to his sons as wicked men, so the people have no strong leadership. Danger from marauders and powerful armies threatens them; Philistines lurk at their borders and frequently invade the land.

Israel has long passed the heady times of Moses and Joshua. Even the memory of charismatic judges, such as Deborah, Gideon, and Jephthah, has faded into the past. The people of Israel are living in an era of transition. From the days of Moses, Yahweh had raised up gifted prophets and warriors in times of need; they spoke for God or led the people to victory against their enemies. Starting with the book of 1 Samuel, we move into the end of that type of ministry and usher in the coronation of King Saul, and later, David.

The transition begins with the weak leadership of Eli. Along with his two evil sons, who use the priestly office for their personal gain, Eli helps push the nation to the verge of disaster. Then God raises up Samuel, and we read of God's preparation for his birth and the lengthy account of his early years. It's a time of spiritual silence when no prophets cry out, "Thus says the Lord!" In fact, 1 Samuel 3:1 says, "The word of the LORD was rare in those days; visions were not widespread."

The book of 1 Samuel begins with Hannah and her husband going to Shiloh for the annual sacrifice (probably Passover). While there, a barren and sorrowful Hannah cries out to God for a child. After the couple returns to their home, her prayer is answered and she bears a child whom she names Samuel.

To that barren woman, the gift of a son is a miracle. The Bible records a number of miraculous births, such as Isaac, Samson, and John the Baptist. Each time the point is that the one who is to achieve much for Israel comes as a gift from the Lord. As 1 and 2 Samuel unfold, the man's achievements don't come so much as a result of his personality or his vast training; he gives himself to God's service, and God honors and uses him.

After Samuel's birth, Hannah vows that as soon as the boy is weaned (scholars think he must have been two or three) she will send him to live at the tent-temple at Shiloh with Eli. An interesting play on words, not obvious in English, sets the significance of this. Chapter 1 ends with the parents taking the boy to Shiloh and leaving him there. The wordplay is in verse 28, where Hannah declares, "Therefore I have lent him to the LORD; as long as he lives, he is given to the LORD." The verb translated "lent" is *shal-al*, and it's similar to the name Samuel (*Shemu-el*). Scholars also point out that the word is almost the same as the Hebrew word for Saul—*sha-ul*. This was probably intentional and meant to be significant to serious readers. The writer wants the people to see the contrast of the king with the faithful prophet-priest. Saul starts well, falters, turns from Yahweh, and finally God rejects him. This statement wants readers to grasp that Samuel is the true Saul, the one lent to God for service. Samuel is the national leader who totally belongs to God and doesn't turn aside. In fact, when the people demand a king, here's how the Bible records the incident:

> But the thing displeased Samuel when they said, "Give us a king to govern us." Samuel prayed to the LORD, and the LORD said to Samuel, "Listen to the voice of the people in all that they say to you; for they have not rejected you, but they have rejected me from being king over them. Just as they have done to me, from the day I brought them up out of Egypt to this day, forsaking me and serving other gods, so also they are doing to you" (1 Samuel 8:6–8).

This sets up readers to realize that Saul is a product of the people, and he will behave like them—willfully and disobediently.

Most significant in the first chapters of the book of 1 Samuel is that the boy, perhaps as young as four years old, receives a call from God. The literal call is repeated four times to make it clear and to erase all doubt from anyone's mind.

The calling of Samuel is simple and straightforward. In the middle of the night Samuel hears his name being called and, assuming it's Eli, rushes into the high priest's bedchamber and cries out, "Here I am, for you called me." The old man says he has not called, and this occurs three times. An editorial comment in the story reads, "Now Samuel did not yet know the LORD, and the word of the LORD had not yet been revealed to him" (1 Samuel 3:7).

After the third interruption of his sleep, the old man "perceived that the LORD was calling the boy" (3:8). He told Samuel to lie down, and if he heard the voice again, he was to say, "Speak, LORD, for your servant is listening" (3:9).

When God awakens the boy a fourth time, Samuel does as Eli told him. With his answer, we peek into the quiet pursuit of a seeking God. The Holy breaks into the child's world and says, "See, I am about to do something in Israel that will make both ears of anyone who hears of it tingle" (3:11). God tells the boy that Eli and his family will be destroyed.

The chapter ends with these words:

> As Samuel grew up, the LORD was with him and let none of his words fall to the ground. And all Israel from Dan to Beersheba [the most northerly and southerly towns inside the borders of Israel] knew that Samuel was a trustworthy prophet of the LORD. The LORD continued to appear at Shiloh, for the LORD revealed himself to Samuel at Shiloh by the word of the LORD. And the word of Samuel came to all Israel. (3:19–4:1)

As Samuel matured, the Israelites increasingly recognized his special role. The Bible says that none of his words "fell to

the ground," which is a Hebraic way of saying that the words
he spoke were wise and practical. The utterance of those words
set to work the forces that would accomplish the divine plan.
The people acknowledged God's presence with Samuel; he
understood their needs. They cry out for guidance, and he
gives them helpful answers.

⁊

What does this lengthy story mean, and why is it so
important that it's recorded in the Bible? For one thing, it's a
fascinating account of God breaking into a life; it's the one
example we have of the encounter of the Holy when we find
no expression of fear, rejection, or concern. The child accepts
this as Yahweh speaking because Eli tells him that it is so.

Although Samuel is never held up as a perfect man, the
account makes it clear that he follows the right path. Later we
read of his own sons not following him; they behave more like
the sons of Eli. He may not be a great parent, even though
he's an outstanding leader and a dedicated disciple.

Because Samuel is the bridge between prophets and kings,
and later provides another transition between Saul and David,
he is often ignored. Yet the Holy pursues Samuel while he was
virtually a toddler. Samuel starts with Yahweh and never
changes or departs from the faith.

When the holy man speaks, he performs the function of a
prophet—being a mouthpiece or speaker for God in dispens-
ing guidance for daily living. From an early age, Samuel not

only obeys implicitly but he also hears and speaks faithfully for God. Nowhere else in the Bible does this kind of accolade appear.

We find several incidents when Yahweh whispers to Samuel. When a young pre-king Saul searches for his lost donkey, Samuel tells him the animal had been found three days earlier. When he goes to anoint Saul's successor, God makes it clear that the first seven sons of Jesse aren't the divinely chosen one. He listens until he hears God say about David, "Rise, and anoint him, for this is the one" (1 Samuel 16:12). There are other stories, each of them reminding us that this man had experienced an encounter with the Holy during childhood. Even as he nears death, his life stands as a memorial of a man who walked with Yahweh all his life. The pattern is there: God speaks; Samuel listens. Yahweh shapes the boy's life, and from that moment on he becomes the voice of God to declare the divine will to the people.

As I've thought of that story, I admire my wife's life, because she's like Samuel in many ways. Since infancy, she has never departed from the faith. I know others who speak of being "cradle Christians." They may not have experienced the relentless chase and the unyielding tenacity that we adult-conversion types speak about, but that doesn't make them lesser Christians. We may have the dramatic stories to share, but they have something perhaps even more precious. They have always known the Loving Father and the Trusted Companion. Like Samuel, they have lived with an assurance and peace that took people like me years to experience.

Did the Holy One pursue them? Of course, even though the wooing began in their earliest days. I'm immensely thankful that God finally lovingly pounced on me and changed my life. But once in a while I wish I had listened to the pursuing voice in childhood.

CHAPTER ELEVEN

FORSAKEN AND REJECTED

The spirit of God came upon Saul in power" (1 Samuel 11:6). Such statements don't appear often in the Old Testament. When they do, however, readers immediately sense that God has prepared a special task. For example, the Spirit came upon Jephthah, and he delivered Israel from their enemies. As we saw in the last chapter, when the Spirit came upon Samson at the end of his life, he received strength to destroy a stone temple with his bare hands. "The spirit of God came upon . . ." is often a mark of the hero or deliverer.

Saul starts out with all the marks of greatness. The Spirit comes upon him after he has been anointed king. He's set to be the magnificent ruler of the nation of Israel. There is, though, a sad ending to Saul's story. The Spirit leaves him. After this we read of a man who, by modern standards, would be called paranoid or bipolar. He's moody and vindictive. He begins trudging downward. At the bottom of that low, depressing path, Saul encounters the Holy. It happens almost at the end of the king's reign as recorded in 1 Samuel 28.

The experience at Endor forms the climax of Saul's life. I don't fully understand this story, and others struggle with it as well. Some cite it as proof that people can commune with the spirits of the dead. Others call the whole thing a deception by the medium (or witch).

I take it literally that the woman contacts the dead spirit of Samuel, and against this there are strong biblical commands. At least four hundred years before King Saul, at the time Moses prepares the people for entrance into the Promised Land, God prohibited this very thing:

> When you arrive in the land the LORD your God is giving you, be very careful not to imitate the detestable customs of the nations living there. For example . . . do not let your people practice fortune-telling or sorcery, or allow them to interpret omens, or engage in witchcraft, or cast spells, or function as mediums or psychics, or call forth the spirits of the dead. Anyone who does these things is an object of horror and disgust to the LORD. (Deuteronomy 18:9–12 NLT)

Despite divine ordinance against contacting the dead, Saul does it. This is the final rebellion; Saul crosses the line. After this, there was no turning back. The Spirit's presence was taken away.

It's difficult to write such words, because I believe strongly in the loving pursuit of the Holy; there are countless biblical passages about God's unceasing, loving persistence. However, I also believe there is a dark side to the picture. The Holy Spirit will only invade and pursue for so long. Fortunately for us, God's grace goes a long, long way. Even so, isn't there a point where we—or anyone—can say, "No! Never! Never!"? Then it's possible for the pursuit of the Holy to stop.

The writer of 1 Samuel records that the vast Philistine armies were rallying for attack: "[Saul] became frantic with fear. He asked the LORD what he should do, but the LORD refused to answer him, either by dreams or by sacred lots or by the prophets" (28:5–6 NLT). In his desperation, Saul takes his drastic, downward step: "Find a woman who is a medium, so I can go and ask her what to do" (28:7 NLT).

Tragic, isn't it? Saul wants a word of guidance so badly that he seeks a method expressly prohibited by the Lord. I suppose it's his way of saying, "If Yahweh won't show me what to do, maybe the devil will."

The king's servants inform him of a medium that lives at Endor; then he disguises himself and visits her at night. He tells her only that he wants to "talk to a man who has died" (28:8). The woman ominously reminds him that it's forbidden to contact the dead and that King Saul "has expelled all the mediums and psychics from the land" (28:9).

Nevertheless, he convinces her to conjure up Samuel, and then the theatrics begin: "When the woman saw Samuel, she screamed, 'You've deceived me! You are Saul!' " (28:12).

Samuel appears and asks, "Why have you disturbed me by calling me back?" (28:15).

"Because I am in deep trouble," [Saul answered]. . . . "The Philistines are at war with us, and God has left me and won't reply by prophets or dreams. So I have called for you to tell me what to do" (28:15).

An interesting question begins Samuel's prediction: "Why ask me if the LORD has left you and has become your enemy?" (28:16). He goes on to prophesy total defeat for Israel and states that Saul and his sons will die in battle. At this, "Saul fell full length on the ground, paralyzed with fright because of Samuel's words" (28:20).

Think of the implications of that situation. Yahweh is now Saul's enemy. The king feels abandoned, absolutely alone and without hope. Saul has crossed the line and has become totally alienated from God—forsaken.

Let's consider this for a moment. To *feel* forsaken isn't the same as *being* forsaken. As any student of God knows, if Saul had only cried out, "Lord, help me," the Holy would have rushed in and embraced him. But he doesn't. He continues on his way, knowing his reign is coming to an end, that his days of life are few, and that his son-in-law David will become king.

He refuses to turn to God.

Forsaken. Saul is destitute, totally alone in the world. He had been a good king in many ways; for instance, he led the people in victorious battles against the Philistines and established a fine army. David respected Saul as the "Lord's anointed," believing that God had raised him up. As such, David would do nothing to bring about the king's defeat.

Saul had brought all the sorrow and chaos on himself.

Forsaken. It's over for Saul. The Holy had pursued him, touched him, shown him the way, and had pleaded with him to follow the truth. As long as Samuel lived, he would have embraced Saul if the king would have changed, but he never did. When Saul commits the grievous sin of disobedience by not killing King Agag of the Amalekites, and Samuel declares that the kingdom has been taken from him, Saul does repent and asks for forgiveness. (See 1 Samuel 15:24–31.)

Here, though, is the fatal flaw in Saul. When confronted with his sin, he readily acknowledges it, and he changes. But he changes for only a short time. His repentance never lasts. That moment could have been a new start, a commitment call for Saul to stir himself, to fall on his knees, to plead for forgiveness. The Bible makes it clear that when such a spirit is present, God embraces the penitent. Yet Saul will not continue to bend.

Forsaken. Cast away from God's presence. Was this really Saul's insistent pulling away from the Holy? Again, I believe that even at Endor, had Saul sought forgiveness, some kind of restoration could have happened, perhaps not to kingship, but to life. Even so, Saul makes no penitent cry; he had already gone over from life to damnation.

As I've thought of the lives of men and women in the Bible, it becomes clear that those who turn their backs on God don't seem to have a powerful experience that destroys their faith. It's more that their faith erodes—a gradual grinding away.

For instance, Demas is one of Paul's traveling companions, mentioned in one of his earlier writings (Colossians 4:14). In Paul's final New Testament authorship comes this statement to Timothy: "Do your best to come to me soon, for Demas, in love with the present world, has deserted me and gone to Thessalonica" (2 Timothy 4:9–10).

Like King Saul, Demas starts well, and because he travels with Paul's entourage and witnesses miracles and healings, we expect him to become one of the great saints of the New Testament. Instead, his faith withers. Even among the exciting and wonderful period of the early spread of the gospel, such things happen.

I grasped this concept during my first year as a believer; I was in my early twenties. I worked with a man named Will, whose last name I've long forgotten. Will was a troubled man, and, although I knew little about God, I held out my hand to him. He listened, accepted what I said, started to attend church, and responded to an invitation to turn to Jesus Christ. Will joined a Bible study class and carried his Bible everywhere. That went on for maybe six months, and Will grew rapidly. His knowledge of the Bible amazed me. He'd read a passage once and understand its meaning. He could turn around and teach profound truths to others in marvelously simple words.

Then he met some longtime companions—men he had once run around with. For about a month I watched helplessly while Will struggled over going back to his old way of life or continuing to follow Jesus Christ. I prayed for him; I counseled him several times, and I asked others to pray.

Eventually Will turned from God. "I'm going back to the way I used to live," he told me. "I'm no good, but at least I know it and I don't have to act like some goody-good person."

I didn't try to argue. The hardness of his face showed me that it would do no good. He had made up his mind. I hugged him, and he tightened up as if to push away my embrace. "Jesus loves you and will always love you," I said, "and you're never too bad for—"

"Shut up! Christianity is a fake! I don't want to hear anything about God or Jesus or the Bible."

I tried to answer, but he shoved me away, cursed me, and said, "I hope I never see you or any of you stupid Christians again."

He never did see me again, although for a few months, I prayed for him every day. Then time, distance, and other matters came up and he became part of a long ago past. About six years later, I was traveling in Ohio and stopped by to visit Burt, a man who had been my friend during those early years of my faith.

"You heard about Will, didn't you?" he asked.

I shook my head.

"Killed himself. Bought a gun and blew his brains out."

We had been sitting in Burt's living room; I got up and

walked outside. A freezing sleet pounded my body, but for several minutes I didn't feel the elements.

Will. Will. Will.

Another forsaken man. I didn't equate him with Saul then, but I do now. Both men had been gifted, and they had so much going for them, but even more, I believe the Holy Spirit had pursued them and touched them. Despite divine invasions and outstretched hands, both had repelled God. They couldn't grasp that there was hope. They looked downward, toward themselves, and saw only misery and pain. They couldn't see beyond who they were, couldn't look past their despicable sinful condition. If only they had clasped the Father's loving hand. If only they could have realized that when we become aware of the evil in our hearts, it's not that we're forsaken, but rather that God's loving embrace enfolds us. He whispers, "I know everything about you, and I still love you."

But those who focus totally on their own lostness can't hear such whispers. They can only think of themselves as forsaken.

For me, King Saul is the most tragic figure of the Old Testament. When we examine his total life, it seems like such a waste. He began as a humble, sincere man. Following is one of the saddest commentaries on the life of any man in the Bible, and especially sad when we realize that this refers to a man who was chosen as the first king of Israel:

So Saul died for his unfaithfulness; he was unfaithful to the LORD in that he did not keep the command of the LORD; moreover, he had consulted a medium, seeking guidance, and did not seek guidance from the LORD. Therefore the LORD put him to death and turned the kingdom over to David son of Jesse. (1 Chronicles 10:13–14)

If only . . . if only.

I thought those words about Will; I think they fit King Saul and Demas as well. If only they could have grasped that even when the Holy One bears down on us, when the pursuit brings anguish, and when we grasp the worst things about ourselves, God still whispers, "I love you."

CHAPTER TWELVE

A POINTING FINGER

Television dramas from *Perry Mason* to *Murder, She Wrote* to *Diagnosis: Murder* all work on a similar plot line. The hour-long show opens with the perpetration of a crime, usually murder. We have a variety of suspects, and the audience isn't supposed to know who did the deed. In the climax, the protagonist, such as Jessica Fletcher, often gathers the involved parties in one room. She carefully explains everything that has gone on during the episode, and then she makes her accusation.

The startled guilty person, taken unaware, wails, "I didn't mean to!" or "I had to do it. He was going to ruin me!" The guilty pay for their crimes, and the sleuth smiles triumphantly.

We know the format; it's as ancient as nascent Jewish history. Second Samuel 12 contains a real-life drama with every bit as much suspense, and finally the pointed finger and the cry, "You are the guilty one!"

⟶

The story leading up to the event is a simple account. King David walks on the rooftop of his house, a flat area, like a balcony or deck today. He spots the beautiful Bathsheba bathing on her rooftop, and lust kicks in. Second Samuel 11 and 12 record the entire episode of their adulterous affair and the aftermath.

Essentially, David's selfishness pushes him to sleep with the wife of Uriah. When she discovers she's pregnant, David calls her husband home from the field of battle on the pretext of seeking news about the war. The king offers Uriah a night with his wife, but the man, true to the warrior's oath to abstain from sexual relations in time of battle, sleeps at the door of the king's house and refuses to visit his own home. Having failed in his first attempt, David gets the man drunk, but Uriah still won't go home. Finally, David sends him back to Commander Joab, along with a letter that instructs the general to set Uriah at the center of the fighting. The ruse succeeds: Uriah's murder not only solves the problem of Bathsheba's pregnancy, but it also allows King David to marry the widow.

Neat solution. Joab follows orders. Uriah dies in battle. David takes Bathsheba to be his wife. He has done wrong and covered it up. *Or has he?*

No one can justify David's actions, because he breaks three of the Ten Commandments: (1) He covets another man's wife; (2) he commits adultery with another man's wife; and (3) he murders Uriah by giving the order to place him in the front lines so that he is killed in battle.

Two actors have significant roles in this recorded event: David is a rich man who has everything he wants, including several wives; Uriah is a poor man with one wife. He's robbed of her and then deliberately put in harm's way. Second Samuel 11 ends with an unrepentant David who enjoys the results of abusing his royal power. He has done the deed, and no one knows. Joab may have suspected the liaison with Bathsheba, but he's David's commander and under the king's authority. It's the kind of crime that the rich and powerful can get away with. *Or can they?*

Chapter 12 sets up the scene for what happens next: "But the thing that David had done displeased the Lord" (11:27). God sends the prophet Nathan to speak to David, and Nathan tells the king a story, which is the most well-known parable in the Old Testament.

Like many of Jesus' stories, Nathan speaks in a clever way to get his listener to judge himself. The difference is that when Jesus teaches, listeners understand the parables as a means of relating a truth and don't take them literally. The effectiveness of Nathan's parable lies precisely in the fact that David believes the prophet is relating a real-life incident.

Think about the setting: David functions not only as king but also as the final court of appeal in matters of justice. We assume that Nathan, Gad, and other prophets regularly discuss current affairs with him and guide him in ruling the country.

Nathan's story is a simple one. A rich man owns great herds of flocks, and a poor man in the same city has only one ewe lamb, the family pet. When a visitor comes to the rich man's house, instead of taking an animal from his own flock, he steals the poor man's only sheep and kills it for the traveler: "Then David's anger was greatly kindled against the man. He said to Nathan, 'As the LORD lives, the man who has done this deserves to die; he shall restore the lamb fourfold, because he did this thing, and because he had no pity'" (2 Samuel 12:5–6).

The story succeeds because David, incensed over the crime, cries out, "That man deserves to die."

Nathan answers David in a voice stronger than Perry Mason could ever have used: "You are the man!" (12:7).

At last! David has slipped away from God and gone his own way. Because no one knew his secrets, he thought he had gotten away with evil. He didn't count on the relentless pursuit.

This is an encounter of David being caught by the Holy— God working through a human instrument; and David stops running. The Spirit could easily have brought direct conviction to David and shown him his sinful ways. But maybe it's too late for God to take that route. Had David taken on the smug, self-righteous attitude of the rich and the powerful?

Because of the series of dreadful deeds, my guess is that

David isn't listening to Yahweh. Instead, he has shut off the quiet, inner way the Holy uses to speak to those who are open. Yet Relentless Grace refuses to stop. God cares immensely about David, and this is evident in the words of the prophet Nathan:

> You are the man! Thus says the LORD, the God of Israel: "I anointed you king over Israel, and I rescued you from the hand of Saul; I gave you your master's house, and your master's wives into your bosom, and gave you the house of Israel and of Judah; and if that had been too little, I would have added as much more." Why have you despised the word of the LORD, to do what is evil in his sight? You have struck down Uriah the Hittite with the sword, and have taken his wife to be your wife, and have killed him with the sword of the Ammonites. (12:7–9)

In measured terms, Nathan pronounces divine judgment on David's sin by foretelling strife, division, and infidelity within the royal household to such a degree that, unlike David's secret sin with Bathsheba, those tragedies will be known to all of Israel.

Here's the point: When we won't hear God's whisper, we have to listen to God's shout. David heeds the thundering voice that lays out his crime in front of the court. What David has done in secret has now become openly known.

David could easily have taken the route of the later King Ahab, who has innocent Naboth falsely accused and murdered so he can steal the man's land. When the prophet Elijah confronts him, the king muses, "So my enemy has found me!" (1 Kings 21:20 NLT).

But David fears God. Quite unlike the television characters that justify or explain away their guilt, David states simply, "I have sinned against the LORD" (12:13). No justifying, no explaining away, because the king faces himself. This not only takes extraordinary courage, but it also says something to us about David and his relationship with God.

Let's look at this encounter with the Holy. David expresses a reality that many of us—even three thousand years later—still don't get. When the Holy says, "You are the man," the king replies, "Yes, I have sinned against you." We tend to think primarily of the people we have harmed, consequently ignoring our offenses against *the personhood of God*. This isn't to imply that David doesn't acknowledge what he has done to Uriah and to Bathsheba and to others. What David does is move to the ultimate issue: It's God he has failed.

Nathan uses strong language in talking to David: "Why have you despised the word of the LORD, to do what is evil in his sight?" (12:9). For the moment, this becomes a scene between only two individuals: Yahweh and David. God cares about the guilty as much as the innocent, but in this moment when the Holy speaks, the emphasis is direct: "It is I—God—whom you have despised," is the effect of the accusation.

David, to his credit, responds exactly to the charge. He has sinned against God. This devout man understands a significant principle: All sin is ultimately against the Holy.

To get the sense of David's response, it helps to read Psalm

51, which has as its heading "A Psalm of David, when the prophet Nathan came to him, after he had gone in to Bathsheba" (NASB). The psalm is a sad, plaintive cry of a man in deep anguish of soul as he pleads for mercy. The first three verses demonstrate this clearly:

> Have mercy on me, O God, because of your unfailing love. Because of your great compassion, blot out the stain of my sins. . . . For I recognize my shameful deeds—they haunt me day and night. Against you, and you alone, have I sinned; I have done what is evil in your sight. (vv. 1, 3–4 NLT)

When we read his words, there is no question that the Holy Pursuer has chased and caught David. He becomes so overwhelmed by his grief over displeasing God that nothing else obscures his vision. When he writes about being haunted day and night, I assume he thinks of the events and the other people involved. But primarily, this man bows his head before the Lord and confesses. Several times in the psalm he pleads for God to forgive him, yet it isn't merely the matter of being forgiven. He wants more: "Oh, give me back my joy again; you have broken me—now let me rejoice. Don't keep looking at my sins" (vv. 8–9 NLT).

The NRSV translates the beginning of verse 9: "Hide your face from my sins."

Relentless grace has trapped the king, and we grasp the depth of his commitment. In the presence of Nathan and others, David admits his evil and wrongdoing. This story emphasizes for me how much we—those who have sinned against others—need some kind of public acknowledgment of our wrongdoing. Today we have gotten into individualism so much that it seems hardly to matter whether we make things right with the injured person(s) as long as we ask God to forgive us. Church leaders no longer take responsibility for guiding and guarding the flock from sin; the church no longer announces forgiveness. That is, we have ignored injunctions such as "Confess your sins to each other and pray for each other so that you may be healed" (James 5:16 NLT).

Let's ponder David's confession. We assume Nathan's accusation comes while the king sits in his court. Others are around him. He publicly acknowledges that he has betrayed the divine trust and the public trust.

We've gone the other way and bypassed this. In all the years I've been a Christian, I know of only one instance of true public confession. In the church where I attended, a woman stood up in the morning worship service and confessed that she and the song leader had been having an affair, that she was pregnant, and that he was the father. She asked the congregation to forgive them both. The man stood up and did the same. The people responded warmly, because they understood that they—the church, God's representatives on earth—had been sinned against as well as the mates of the two people.

When the woman confessed, she said that she did so because it's what the Bible taught and that she needed the forgiveness of the congregation as well as the forgiveness of God. For her, as with David, public repentance holds hands with private repentance. Psalm 51 exemplifies this. David penned those words from what reads like deep depression. He wanted restoration, but seemed to struggle with accepting it.

We can also learn from the situation with David that when the Holy confronts us, the pain may be so great that it may seem as if there is no forgiveness. It appears that the morning will never break again, and that it will always be midnight: "Do not cast me away from your presence, and do not take your holy spirit from me" (51:11).

If David had examined this situation logically and objectively, he would know he was already forgiven. After all, God is love, and the Bible repeatedly assures us of forgiveness, restoration, and even joy. In the midst of his anguish, however, David can't feel this hope or assurance. The Holy bears down hard, and a finger points, accusing, "You are the one! You are that man."

Maybe the Holy confronts us so powerfully in order that we will have no doubts about the level of our sinfulness or the magnitude of our need. At times we may need to be brought so low that only by looking upward can we have peace once again. In those times, we clasp the invisible hand of grace, knowing that we can accept it only through tear-filled eyes. God has pursued us; God has caught us.

CHAPTER THIRTEEN

AFTER THE HIGH

The first time I became aware of the phenomenon of "the high" was after I had been a believer for about two years. Shirley and I belonged to the 400-member Lakeshore Tabernacle in Kenosha, Wisconsin. That summer, nearly fifty young people went away for a retreat. Every one of them came back glowing and rejoicing. They went to various people and asked forgiveness. In front of the entire congregation they spoke about their renewed lives.

"I'll never be the same again," the first person said. Then she told of the changes that had already taken place. At least four others who spoke after her said essentially the same thing. Renewed. Invigorated. Committed. Dedicated.

After a month, however, their behavior had returned to that of the pre-retreat days. I remember one girl saying that she was absolutely miserable: "This is the worst I've ever felt in my life." She questioned what she had experienced and then decided that something was wrong with her.

One boy, who had been extremely hyped after the experience, left the church within weeks. "It's just not real," he said. "I got my emotions stirred up or something, but I just don't believe any of that anymore."

Since then I've seen this kind of thing occur many times. People have what we often refer to as mountaintop experiences. They are different and vow they'll never go back to their old ways. Sometimes they do have a drastic lifestyle shift. Far more often, however, they return to their former life, or at least shift backward enough that they're filled with condemnation or depression.

"I felt so wonderful two weeks ago," I heard someone say after a spiritual high. "Now I feel lower than a snake's belly."

Maybe this is just the way our emotions work. Or maybe we have the experience, and then comes the reality test. Perhaps it's an opportunity for an encounter with the Holy, a pursuit that takes place in the gloomy valley of despair and not on the mountaintop of joy.

An incident in the Bible illustrates this. In the waning days of the divided nation of Israel, the prophet Elijah appears. This awesome man has no fear. He confronts sin and rebukes King Ahab and his wife, Jezebel. At one point he declares that there will be no rain until he says so. For the next three and a half years, Israel lives in drought.

One day God tells Elijah that it's time for the rain to return. The prophet then faces King Ahab and challenges him to a kind of duel on top of Mount Carmel. In this well-known story, 450 prophets of the heathen god Baal and 400 prophets of Asherah have a showdown with Yahweh and his prophet Elijah. On one side of the mountain, the prophets of Baal prepare a sacrifice and pray for their god to burn up the carcass. From morning until noon they plead and scream, but nothing happens. Taunted by Elijah, they cry louder and cut themselves, yet nothing changes.

Finally comes Elijah's turn. He has people dig a trench around the altar and then empties twelve water-filled jars on the sacrifice "so that the water ran all around the altar, and filled the trench also with water" (1 Kings 18:35). Elijah prays for God to answer: "Then the fire of the LORD fell and consumed the burnt offering, the wood, the stones, and the dust, and even licked up the water that was in the trench" (18:38).

Stunned, the people fall down and worship Yahweh. Elijah has the evil prophets seized and put to death. Afterward he announces that the rain will return. The Bible then records a short scene of Elijah praying seven times until a cloud appears. That's the sign he awaits, and soon the heavens open and rain fills the land.

What a glorious time for this great prophet! He is not only literally on the mountaintop, but emotionally it must be a high point in his life. He has confronted the king and all the evil prophets, and God performs a miracle. As a result, Israel worships the true Lord.

Then Elijah comes down from the mountain and goes into a deep funk. This is how the Bible sets it up:

Ahab told Jezebel all that Elijah had done, and how

he had killed all the prophets with the sword. Then Jezebel sent a messenger to Elijah, saying, "So may the gods
do to me, and more also, if I do not make your life like
the life of one of them by this time tomorrow." Then he
was afraid; he got up and fled for his life, and came to
Beer-sheba. (19:1–3)

Amazing! The great prophet has just scored an outstanding victory over the priests of Baal, followed by a miracle of
torrential rain. It has not rained for three and a half years, and
yet after he prays the rain returns. What a day of wonders!
This is the man who has withstood the powers of evil and
won. He has thwarted the king of the land.

After he comes down from the mountain, however, things
change. Fear clutches him when he receives a threatening message from the queen. At first this seems unbelievable; he has
been hunted for all those months during the drought and
hasn't been afraid.

Has the danger increased any? Not likely. Before Mount
Carmel, the military combs the country seeking him, and
Ahab wants him killed. After he scores a victory at Carmel,
how could the threats get worse?

The change, obviously, must be within Elijah. *He is afraid*.
He sinks into depression. Maybe those soaring moments set
expectations too high to sustain. After an emotional high, we
often plummet quickly and then find it difficult to understand
how we could fall so far so fast.

That's what happens to Elijah. He's human, and he
responds emotionally. One of the ways to respond to fear is to

run, which is exactly what he does. After he's alone in the wilderness, the biblical record says, "He himself went a day's journey into the wilderness, and came and sat down under a solitary broom tree. . . . 'It is enough; now, O LORD, take away my life, for I am no better than my ancestors'" (19:4).

He then stretches out and sleeps, only to be awakened later by an angel who provides food and water. He sleeps a second time, and again the divine messenger brings nourishment. Then Elijah walks all the way to Mount Horeb and hides inside a cave.

That's where the encounter with the Holy takes place. First, God asks him why he is there. The prophet's defensive, perhaps whining, answer reads, "I have been very zealous for the LORD, the God of hosts; for the Israelites have forsaken your covenant, thrown down your altars, and killed your prophets with the sword. I alone am left, and they are seeking my life, to take it away" (19:10).

Whatever the cause for the prophet's dejection, he is so low he believes, at least for the moment, that he's the only faithful believer left on earth. He's mistaken, and perhaps he knows this intellectually. However, emotionally, he is so dismayed and depressed, he grasps nothing beyond his fear of Queen Jezebel's wrath and his sense of being abandoned. He feels friendless and alone.

This is where the Holy encounters Elijah—at his dark moment of discouragement. This is the place where he's too low to look upward. This is an instance of the relentless pursuit—not just when we fail or sin or go astray, but just as much when we're depressed, estranged, or helpless.

This is one of those times that the psalmist speaks of God's *hidden face*, a time when the person knows of the Lord's presence but can't feel it. At its most extreme, it becomes what St. John of the Cross referred to as the dark night of the soul. We long for a word, a miracle, a verse—anything to reassure us that the Holy Spirit is with us. It's worse for us when our friends speak of their victories, and at church we hear of the Holy Spirit who always answers prayers. If that's the case, we begin to reason, something must be wrong with us. And the more we ponder it, the worse it gets. We confess our sins, perhaps repeatedly, and search our hearts for any failures or small acts of disobedience. No matter what we say or do, the darkness prevails.

I can't explain these times, but I know that if we seek to move forward with God, this is part of the plan—we have to have dark nights along with bright days. We step forward in darkness and have no assurance that we're even going in the right direction. But if we hang on and wait, and that's usually all we can do, the Holy breaks into our lives once again.

❧

I can write about all of this from experience. For a period of eighteen months, beginning in 1996, I felt as if nothing but darkness filled my life. (I describe this more fully in my book *Seeking God's Hidden Face: When God Seems Absent* [InterVarsity, 2001].) For weeks I cried out, "Where are you,

God? What's wrong with me? Where have I failed? Have I sinned?" I confessed and re-confessed sins, but nothing changed.

Even though I knew I wasn't the first person to ask such questions, that didn't make the dilemma any easier. During those months, I discovered that this emptiness becomes a vital part of the growing process. It wasn't pleasant, and I hated going through it. Worse, only in hindsight did I value the difficult times I had gone through.

God simply didn't respond to my deepest cries and longings. Many days I wondered how I could keep going onward when I encountered only silence. It's not that I demanded emotional jolts or miraculous answers, but I longed for that sense of God's presence. "Just a whisper, God," I pleaded.

Trying to explain this experience reminds me of walking outside on a starless night. We call it starless because we can see only dark, ugly clouds covering the horizon. Yet we know that beyond the thick murkiness the stars shine as brightly as they do on any other night. Our eyes simply can't penetrate the darkness.

For a time we're forced to live in lunar eclipse, a period of unrelenting gloom. This goes on so long that it seems like a way of life; it gets tougher and more discouraging to keep on walking through the dark, forlorn night. We know we need to go forward, but we feel as if we've lost our bearings and aren't sure which path leads ahead. No matter where we turn in our search for divine direction, we find only a silent emptiness. There's nothing to see, because God's face remains deliberately hidden from us. It may be only a cloud of separation, but it feels like a wall of solid steel that shuts us off.

Even when we sense divine strategy at work, it doesn't help much. We still want a heavenly response to our prayers. We don't rely on emotion, but at least once in a while we want to "feel" God's presence or be infused with a sense of certainty that everything's all right in our relationship. Can't we have just a tiny nod of assurance that the Spirit is orchestrating the night music? Even if God's not taking an active role, can't we get a hint of guidance? a gentle nudge? a whisper? Instead, we encounter only silence, emptiness, and more of the lunar eclipse.

Of course, God is there. In these times, our awareness and our emotions don't square with our theological bearings. As far as we're concerned, God just isn't there for us, and we can't do anything to change the situation. Despite our agonized groanings and pleadings, we receive no answer, and we can't force the Holy Spirit to act. For all practical living purposes, God simply isn't present.

After a year and a half, the Holy broke into my life—softly. I had reached the point where I had begun to believe that the Holy Spirit would never speak to me again; I would be forced to live without God's face smiling upon me. The final morning of a writers' conference in Colorado, I went out for my daily run, an hour before daylight. Words can't explain what happened, but as I raced along the road, the Spirit whispered in what I call "that silent voice." I knew—and it was that deep, inner knowledge I couldn't explain, and yet I didn't have the least doubt. God was getting ready to smile on me once again.

Within days the spiritual light blazed, and I sensed God's smiling face. It was the first time I had any experiential sense of what Elijah went through in his cave: for more than three years he has given himself, seemingly alone, and has battled the powers of evil. Now he's burned out and empty.

In his weakness, Elijah is ready for Yahweh to break in and speak, and it's breathtaking when God encounters him. As Elijah stands at the cave entrance, his senses are assaulted by a wind of terrifying force, then by an earthquake, and finally by a fire. In the Bible, those natural forces are traditional signs of the holy presence (see Psalm 18:7–10; 29:3–9), but here they are merely noise and movement.

After the violent disturbances of nature comes a divine manifestation. He speaks, but it's one of those Hebrew expressions that scholars find difficult to translate. They translate it a "still small voice," or "the soft whisper," or "the sound of sheer silence."

Whatever it is that happens, Elijah discerns that Yahweh is present. This is God, the voice of silence, and the voice that has no sound. This is the Relentless, Loving, Grace-Giving Holy One breaking into his life. The language sounds much like the experience of mystics—those who are keyed in to inner action and nonverbal nuances, and that revel in the silence and hear in solitude.

I'm not a mystic, but I've learned that silence is an important element in our relationship with God. Those who are so in tune with silence that they readily hear the holy whispering voice are the mystics, the introverts, and the inwardly directed. Others, like me, who are more outwardly directed, prefer to hear and see God in the wind, the earthquake, and the fire.

I wonder if that's not the type of person Elijah was—the effusive extrovert? Although he's usually depicted as a hermit type, I suspect he's more like those of us who thrive and are energized by movement and activity. We can handle persecution and opposition. We can argue or discuss our theology. It's the silence that intimidates us. It's the silence we fear. We seek and expect to find the Holy Spirit in the happenings around us: the worship experience, the service activities, and anything that demands high-energy participation. We don't like quiet, and we fill our homes, offices, and even our cars with noise. Televisions, stereos, cell phones boom at us. We say we tune them out, but I suspect that one of the reasons we have all that ruckus is because we fear emptiness—the nothingness of silence. However, sometimes in our lives we're confronted with silence, and when that happens, the Holy can break through. We stop and listen, and that moment becomes another triumph for the Divine Pursuer.

God does get through to Elijah. This time it happens at

Mount Horeb, a different mountain. The Holy slips in quietly, softly, and whispers.

That's the hard way for many of us to hear. It may also be the way we need to hear—a fresh approach, a breaking in of divine holiness because it is different. It's not the usual manner in which we sense the Spirit ministering to us. It's an alternative mountaintop experience. We sense that we have no outward events to stir our emotions; we're cut off from everyone. No one is there with us. Just God.

Maybe that's why the cave in the wilderness is so important. Elijah has no one else, no other voice or sound to listen to. Now the Holy can break through, culminating the long pursuit.

Such moments can become joyful experiences when we realize that grace never lets go of us. Maybe our best moments can come to us when we meet the Relentless God afresh in the noiseless moments of life.

CHAPTER FOURTEEN

UNHOLY
ATTITUDES

Most nonbelievers know the story of Jonah and the great sea creature, but they don't know much else about the book. Believers can fairly accurately describe the fish-swallowing incident, but they rarely understand the purpose of the book. What's the message of the book of Jonah?

It's quite simple: God's love is universal.

Perhaps I should say that it's simple for us; it wasn't simple for ancient Jews to grasp. They were the chosen people. For them, this fact could only mean that others—non-Jews—were un-chosen. If the chosen people were loved, then those of other nations were despised. If they were the objects of Yahweh's salvation, obviously the heathen peoples represented divine wrath at work. When we read a dozen times that the Jews were special, designed as the people of God, it becomes a drastic step of faith to believe that God's compassion embraced other nations as well.

Jonah is an individual, but he also represents the mindset of an ancient people. For instance, he understands Yahweh's love and compassion a little more than we might give some others credit for. God commands him to go to the capital of the Assyrian empire, Nineveh. He refuses to go, even though the command is to preach their destruction. The beginning of this slim book of forty-eight verses reads: "Now the word of the LORD came to Jonah, son of Amittai, saying, 'Go at once to Nineveh, that great city, and cry out against it; for their wickedness has come up before me'" (1:1–2).

The command is clear: Preach destruction and punishment for their wickedness. Tell them they're going to die for their sins. That sounds like a rather wonderful message for a Jew to deliver. After all, the chosen people seek the destruction of "God's enemies."

Jonah grasps the message and its implications. When he finally gets there and delivers the divinely commissioned word, something happens (exactly what he thought would happen): the people listen, turn from their sins, and beg for forgiveness. After the people of Nineveh repent, an extremely angry Jonah moans, "O LORD! Is not this what I said while I was still in my own country? That is why I fled to Tarshish at the beginning; for I knew that you are a gracious God and merciful, slow to anger, and abounding in steadfast love, and ready to relent from punishing" (4:2).

Jonah doesn't like what God wants him to do. Apparently,

he intuited that if he preached destruction, the people would repent and change their ways. If that happened, Yahweh would relent and not destroy them. If he didn't go to Nineveh and didn't preach, they would continue with their wickedness, divine wrath would flow, and they would die. "Good enough for them," I can hear the prophet saying, gleefully, as he tries to run away from his calling.

The story of Jonah reminds me of an incident from my own life. While we were living in Kenya, working as missionaries among the Luo tribe, I became acquainted with several East Indians, all of whom were Hindu or Muslim. As they got to know me and let me talk to them about Jesus Christ, they also asked questions. Excitedly, I told another missionary about how things were going.

"God didn't call me to the Asians," he sniffed. "God called me to reach the Africans."

For several seconds, I reeled from the impact of his words. Then I protested, "That's not true. God has called us to all people."

I still recall my shock over such an attitude. I've since realized that this approach isn't all that unusual. A counterpart is to say, "God only cares about good people." It's the mindset that if we change or become righteous enough God will accept us.

I'm reminded of a friend named Jim, who was once told

by a serious believer, "You don't drink or swear. It would be so easy for you to become a Christian." However, his moral behavior didn't make it any easier when he finally faced his need for "something more" in life. What he didn't do meant nothing; what he needed was a change of heart, not of habit.

Jonah needed an encounter with the Holy. I think he actually has two instances of the Holy Pursuer on his trail in this story. After being commanded to go to the city of Nineveh, Jonah boarded a ship and tried to run away. A storm rushed in, and the sailors decided that the turbulence was because of Jonah, so they cast him overboard, and the tumult subsided.

A huge fish swallowed the prophet, and he spent three days inside that sea creature (see 1:17). The entire second chapter of the book, written in poetic form, is a prayer of repentance. In that place, the prophet stopped running. God did not only catch him, but he was trapped inside the fish. Something wonderful happened to the man—or more accurately, began to happen when he was at his lowest point—stuck inside a fish and not sure if he would live. He faced death and should have died in the sea. From inside the fish, he gave thanks to God and said, "As my life was ebbing away, I remembered the LORD; and my prayer came to you" (2:7).

This is the repentance, the change-of-heart experience of a man who felt no compassion for his enemies. After the ordeal in the fish, "The word of the LORD came to Jonah a second

time, saying, 'Get up, go to Nineveh, that great city, and pro-
claim to it the message that I tell you' " (3:1–2). This time
and without any argument, Jonah went as directed. He
reached the city and boldly announced, "In forty days, God
will destroy you all."

The people repented, all the way down from the king, who
made a decree for every person to obey. They even declared a
fast for both people and animals. Everyone was covered with
sackcloth, an outward sign of repentance. The king reasoned,
"Who knows? God may relent and change his mind; he may
turn from his fierce anger, so that we do not perish" (3:9). God
heard their cries and withheld the promised destruction.

That's where most people stop reading, at the end of chapter 3. But there is another powerful incident, focused once
again on Jonah. How did the prophet react to divine mercy in
sparing the people? Here's how chapter 4 begins: "But this
was very displeasing to Jonah, and he became angry" (4:1). He
became so distraught and furious over the merciful acceptance
of the pagans, he begged God to take his life.

The book ends with a brief story, a kind of object lesson.
If we spoke of Jonah's reaction, we'd probably say that he was
angry with Yahweh; that he became depressed and then suicidal. He pleaded for death. I suspect it was also a way of
bargaining or demanding that God destroy the people and
honor the wrathful prophet's message of doom.

Jonah decided to sit out the forty days and wait for the
city to be destroyed. The account then reads: "The LORD God
appointed a bush, and made it come up over Jonah, to give

shade over his head, to save him from his discomfort; so Jonah was very happy about the bush" (4:6). At dawn, however, God sent a worm to eat the plant, and it withered. When the sun arose, Jonah sat on the hill, unprotected from the heat.

This then becomes the lesson. God asked (paraphrased), "Are you angry about the bush?"

"I sure am, and I deserve to be. It protected me from the sun, but now it's gone and—"

"Wait a minute. You didn't do anything to make that bush grow, did you? It just came up in the middle of the night and covered you."

"Yes, that's true, but—"

"And it protected you from the sun."

"Yes—"

"Then that same plant died as quickly as it appeared. And you're angry about that whole thing, aren't you?"

"I certainly am."

"Poor, poor Jonah. Your heart can fill with anger over such a little thing as a bush that spurted growth overnight and then died, but you're not concerned about the lives of 120,000 people."

The loving Creator hammered it home by adding, "If you can get so distraught over a bush, why shouldn't I be distraught over 120,000 souls who don't even know right from wrong?"

What do the message and person of Jonah say to us, the modern readers? Isn't this an encounter with the Holy? Isn't this a powerful jab at our self-righteousness? at our indifference? at the hardness of our hearts?

Isn't this a way for the Holy Pursuer to break into our lives with an in-your-face approach? Sometimes this confrontational tone is exactly what we need to enable us to hear the heavenly voice.

These stinging words must have trapped Jonah. We don't know what happened afterward, because the book ends. The book of Jonah lays out the insignificance of the man's anger and the stupidity of his position. Then readers must make up their own mind about what follows.

If the Holy broke into Jonah's life at that moment and used it as an instrument to break into the lives of the Jews during that period, what did God want to do in their lives?

At the beginning of the chapter, I said the story points out the universality of God's love. Divine love and compassion extends to the entire world, excluding no one. What Christian wouldn't smile and say "Amen" to that bit of theology? Yet when it comes to practical, day-to-day living, I'm amazed at the ways in which we deny the message God drilled home to Jonah.

*

The most blatant way we deny God's universal love is through racism. We like feeling smug and superior to someone else.

When I was a boy growing up in Iowa, I went to school with African-American kids; not many, but a few. The prejudice I saw wasn't against them, but aimed at Mexicans who had settled into the poorest part of town. Many of them didn't have electricity or running water. I saw many prejudicial acts toward them. My wife grew up in Illinois, and the brunt of the prejudice there was against Native Americans.

What about gender prejudice? I used to get daily e-mail jokes that I loathed, putting women down. Now I'm getting many male-bashing jokes, which I find just as distasteful. I wonder if that's not something many of us need to face in an encounter with the Holy.

Perhaps the biggest kind of prejudice we need to confront is in comparing ourselves with others. "I've never killed or defrauded anyone," I've heard people say in defense of their way of life, and I've heard those words in the church too.

If we look down on those people—the ones we ignore or dislike—and talk only to "our kind" of people, are we really any different from Jonah and the Jews of his day?

Is it possible that Jonah's divine encounter is to open our eyes and hearts to grasp a vital message? My answer is a resounding yes, and that message is "Every soul is important." The prophet became angered over such an insignificant thing as a bush that died, but he felt no compassion for the 120,000 people against whom he had prophesied doom.

The Jonah story reminds me of an event that happened in Kenya. We regularly bought meat from Ogada, the local butcher. Three times a week, he slaughtered and skinned a cow and hung it inside his small store. Customers came in, pointed to the portion they wanted, and Ogada cut it off. Because my wife bought meat for the girls' dormitory, we not only bought larger amounts but Ogada often saved the more tender cuts for us.

I had been going to his shop for more than a year before he began to talk to me. He had never insulted me, but until then I had been unable to get more than the customary greeting from him. Then an evangelist began to hold worship services about half a mile from Ogada's home. One Sunday, the loud, joyful singing made him curious enough to attend. To his surprise, he enjoyed the experience and kept going back. Eventually Ogada became a believer.

One day when I visited the mud-and-thatch church, Ogada greeted me with a big smile, an outstretched hand, and the greeting of "Brother." He told me that Jesus had changed his life and that he was now a Christian.

Then he told me about himself. His father had worked for the British during the colonial days and had been badly treated. As a result, Ogada had built up hatred against all whites. He didn't show any evidence of hatred toward me when I came into his shop, but "I hated you the way I hated all white foreigners," he told me.

Then Ogada changed; God changed him. "Now I love you

as a brother," he beamed. He embraced me and kept asking me to forgive him. Of course, I did.

Just before I left him that day, he said, "You are my brother. Your skin may be white, but inside your heart is as black as mine."

His words stunned me. In some way I could not have comprehended, the Holy had pursued the man through years of anger, bitterness, and hatred. Not only had the pursuit ended with Ogada's believing in Jesus Christ, but he also received a new attitude.

That's a major work of the Holy!

That's the message Jonah didn't get.

Or perhaps he did get it. That may be why he wrote the short letter, exposed his hardness and shallow thinking, and ended the book so abruptly. It might have been his divinely inspired way of saying, "I didn't understand the universality of God's love. I had to face my most trying circumstances before the Holy broke into my life, pursued me, and changed me."

Maybe Jonah is saying to us today, "As you read this, perhaps you, too, will see how much we run from the Holy. Doesn't it make more sense to give in? to welcome others? to embrace those we haven't loved?"

If we can internalize that message, we just might have encountered the Holy ourselves.

CHAPTER FIFTEEN

No Longer Running Away

Isn't *No Longer Running Away* a presumptuous title for this chapter? Well, it's an attempt to point to my best intention. Unlike Jacob, I want to be able to say, "God was here all the time, and I know it."

I'm not at that place in my life yet. I still run—not as fast, not as far, not as often—but it's still breaking away and asserting my own will.

For example, by e-mail I shared a chapter of a book with two writer friends. I didn't want them to edit or tell me how they would have written it, and I added, "It's still a rough draft, so don't pay any attention to misspellings." I had a specific purpose in mind and asked, "Does the chapter do the job?" Both edited the chapter, pointing out my typos, and offered generous advice for my writing and for my self-improvement. In anger, I typed a terse response.

Just before the mouse on my computer clicked "send," I

felt a slight inner tugging. It wasn't a shout, no Bible verse popped into my head, and guilt didn't overwhelm me. It felt more like an undefined noise in the background, which I ignored.

Within a nanosecond after my computer showed the message had left, that undefined tugging became a clanging noise, and I admitted it: I had been wrong, and I agonized over what I had done.

After asking God to forgive me, I sent a new message asking their forgiveness for my angry, rash tone. I didn't apologize for the message, only the spirit in which I had sent it. Both forgave me.

Perhaps that doesn't read like a highly significant story. At least it doesn't come across with the word SIN written in capital letters. But it was sin. I had pulled away from God's hand, and Cec Murphey was on the run again. But thanks to the relentless pursuit of the Holy Spirit, I had a divine encounter.

I wish I hadn't sent the angry e-mail. Next time, perhaps I'll be sensitive enough so the Spirit can warn me that I don't need to retaliate or that I can wait to reply when I'm calm.

In little ways, then, I still run, and God still pursues. On my best days, I sense Jesus walking beside me in intimate fellowship. On other days, however, I'm hiding behind well-crafted fig leaves and dreading the divine scrutiny.

Too often I've become aware of the Pursuing God only after I've encountered hindrances, or my brilliant, well-conceived plans have failed to materialize. Those disappointments force me to cry out, "I surrender, and I repent! You're in control, God."

Too often I've felt like Joshua just before the Israelites moved against Jericho and the armed soldier confronts him. Perhaps he saw himself as *only* the leader of the chosen people. Or did he perceive himself as the one in control and assume that Israel's victories would depend on him? That's how I think I would have felt. Did the "man" appear to make it clear that Joshua was Yahweh's *servant*, and there is only one commander?

In my zeal, I've sometimes ignored or shrugged off the gentle touch of the Pursuing God. I haven't done this consciously, and I think I speak for many of us who hunger for a deeper relationship. We don't intentionally take control or deny the sound of feet clattering behind us. Sometimes God surprises us and stands in front of us as if to say, "Stop! I won't let you go in this direction."

I've been like pagan Balaam, the Old Testament prophet, who either couldn't or didn't want to see God blocking the path. This is my ongoing dilemma of advocating and urging people to live a life that I haven't yet attained.

I keep asking: *What can I say that will help others stop running and end the pursuit? Who am I to try to tell Christians things that will help them prepare themselves for the next episode of the divine pursuit when I can't even fully do it myself? What gives me the right to set myself up as a divine messenger?*

I'm still trudging onward, and the spot marked "spiritual perfection" looks farther away than ever. In fact, the longer I'm on the heavenly road, the more it feels as if Someone stealthily moves the marker over the next ridge.

I found the courage to write this book because of something my friend, the late Ken Bennett Sr. said: "We all teach beyond our reach." He meant we perceive the reality, and we talk about what we've only begun to experience.

As I ponder his words once again, I realize that I have to speak from where I am.

Like other Christians, I also need to remind myself that, despite what we do, our Savior hasn't given up on us—it's a love that just won't quit. This often requires a holy pursuit before we stop our frenzied activities and turn more fully to God. The divine wooing comes in a multitude of ways. We don't like to think of God breaking into our daily patterns— and especially not that God has to break in. We prefer to speak of our Savior replying, responding, or helping when we cry out in our times of need. We like the religious idea of our praying and the Spirit answering our cries. "I sought God's will" or "I prayed for guidance" are nice, simple explanations.

Yet basic to Christian theology is that human sin created an unbreachable gulf between an imperfect humanity and a perfect divinity. No matter how hard we try, we can't earn or demand God's love. Salvation, grace, kindness, understanding, and all the other good gifts come to us because God breaks through and invades our sinful, imperfect human world and pursues us until we stop. To put it simplistically, God reaches *down* because we can't reach *up* high enough to make the connection.

In the Incarnation we have the most powerful form of divine pursuit. Christ laid aside Godhood and was born as a helpless infant named Jesus. As he grew, he lived a perfect human life, suffered, was crucified, died, and was buried. God raised that perfect man from the dead, and he later returned to heaven to become once again the Divine Christ. This means more than Jesus dying for our sins. The Savior pursued humanity inside our finite world to demonstrate God's infinite unrelenting quest for everyone. It's "Love That Wilt Not Let Me Go," as the old hymn declares. It's the promise clearly stated in John 3:16. It's the cry of Matthew 11:28: "Come to me, all you that are weary and are carrying heavy burdens, and I will give you rest."

All of this leads me to the powerful conclusion that God has called each of us to be like Jesus—but that's not the total message. To become like our Savior and our Role Model means accepting ourselves as we are, and allowing the Holy One to change us. Once we accept that God pursues us relentlessly, and always does this for our good, we can focus on the pragmatic reason: God pursues us as our call to obedience.

Just that simple.

Just that difficult.

Despite my lack of spiritual attainment, the Bible and my own experience convince me that God's overwhelming desire is to push us to face ourselves. In that self-scrutiny, we can discover the relentless love of the Savior who constantly reaches toward us. In those moments, we realize that the Holy Spirit chases us down every hallway, through every doorway, and meets us at every intersection. These pursuits flow from a passionate desire to embrace us and enrich our lives.

As soon as we stop running and lift our arms to be enclosed by the extended divine embrace, our lives become different. We'll look the same and probably keep the same jobs and attend the same church, but inside, we'll be different. We'll know we've changed, even if we assume no one else notices.

Our task isn't to become famous, wealthy, influential, or indispensable. God doesn't call us to teach the largest Sunday school class or to be the number one deacon in our congregation. The holy pursuit is to make us obedient.

We may commit ourselves to doing small, unseen tasks for God, and no one will ever commend us. When I was a pastor, we had a church custodian named Wilburn Williams, who was paid for thirty hours of work each week, but he easily put in fifty. Although I appreciated it, I never gave Wilburn the public thanks he deserved. I wish I had.

Dan Sumerour wasn't much of a communicator, but whenever anyone in our congregation was hospitalized, he and his wife, Ann, went there immediately. They stayed out of the way and ministered more to the family than the patient simply by listening. The most they ever received was a verbal thanks or a handwritten note, but I don't think they minded.

If we're obedient, others may receive credit for our labors. For instance, as a ghostwriter for several famous people, I've had to battle my commitment to obedience. It hurt when a celebrity received the accolades for books that changed lives and he or she never mentioned my name.

That's the object of the divine pursuit. It leads us to say, "Speak, LORD, for your servant is listening" (1 Samuel 3:10). When we say *listening*, we imply that we'll then carry out whatever God asks of us.

We also need to be able to understand (and we can't explain to others) that because we were lovingly pursued and warmly embraced, the Holy Spirit changes us. We become different. We're not like other people. We can't be.

For some of us that means we learn to rejoice when God ties our tongues, chains our hands, or closes our eyes to the way others behave. We can no longer judge others or consider them less spiritual. After all, who are we to make such pronouncements? We know that we have to be faithfully obedient to what our loving Savior says to us. God places spiritual blinders on us so we can perceive only what lies straight ahead. We can't focus on others' flaws and shortcomings. If we do peek at their actions or try to compare ourselves, the Spirit lovingly chastises us and asks, "Who are you to condemn God's servants? They are responsible to the Lord, so let him tell them whether they are right or wrong" (Romans 14:4 NLT).

The Holy Spirit also rebukes us for our hastily chosen words or our careless humor that hurts another's feelings.

Once we face the unrelenting pursuit by God in our lives, we become aware that we're no longer running but walking along with the Infinite Sovereign, who has chosen our path as well as our actions. God may not explain a thousand things that puzzle us or make clear why bad things happen. However, once we stop running and offer ourselves as love slaves, God's embrace wraps us in a jealous love and hugs us tightly. We'll discover blessings that we can't express, much less shout about, to others.

This is what makes the encounter with the Relentless God worthwhile.

CECIL MURPHEY has authored or coauthored over eighty books. He has earned master's degrees in theology and education, taught school, mentored other writers, and served as a missionary in Africa. He and his family live in Atlanta, Georgia.

Thank you for selecting a book from
BETHANY HOUSE PUBLISHERS

Bethany House Publishers is a ministry of Bethany Fellowship International, an interdenominational, nonprofit organization committed to spreading the Good News of Jesus Christ around the world through evangelism, church planting, literature distribution, and care for those in need. Missionary training is offered through Bethany College of Missions.

Bethany Fellowship International is a member of the National Association of Evangelicals and subscribes to its statement of faith. If you would like further information, please contact:

Bethany Fellowship International
6820 Auto Club Road
Bloomington, MN 55438 USA

www.bethfel.org